GROSSET'S

FRENCH

PHRASE BOOK
AND
DICTIONARY

by Charles A. Hughes

A GD/PERIGEE BOOK

OTHER BOOKS IN THIS SERIES:

Grosset's German Phrase Book
and Dictionary for Travelers

Grosset's Italian Phrase Book
and Dictionary for Travelers

Grosset's Spanish Phrase Book
and Dictionary for Travelers

Perigee Books
are published by
The Putnam Publishing Group
200 Madison Avenue
New York, New York 10016

LC: 78-144060
ISBN 0-399-50794-9

First Perigee printing, 1982
Printed in the United States of America

Seventh Impression

CONTENTS

Introduction..................... v
Tips on Pronunciation and Accent.... vi
Salutations and Greetings............ 1
The Weather...................... 4
General Expressions............... 8
Emergencies.....................13
Signs and Notices.................16
Numbers, Time and Dates...........19
Changing Money..................29
Customs........................32
At the Hotel.....................35
Using the Telephone...............40
Getting Around by Taxi and Bus.....43
Eating and Drinking...............47
Menu Reader.....................57
Shopping........................61
Getting Around by Automobile......72
Getting Around by Train............82
Getting Around by Ship and Plane....86
Health..........................91
Sightseeing......................97
Dictionary......................103

INTRODUCTION

In this phrase book for travel in the French-speaking countries, we have tried to incorporate features that will make it convenient and easy for you to use in actual situations. Every phrase and word is translated into proper French and then respelled to guide you in its pronunciation.

The book is also "programmed" to help you with two of the basic problems of the novice in a language — an inability to comprehend the spoken word and a certain hesitancy in speaking out. To solve the first problem, questions have been avoided, to the extent possible, in the phrases. When they could not be avoided, they have been worded so that a yes or no answer may be expected. And sometimes, when even this solution is impossible, the anticipated answer is given. To solve the problem of hesitancy, the contents of the book have been arranged so that a minimal command of the basic phrases, salutations, weather, numbers, time, statements of need and desire, may be acquired in the first sections. The pronunciation guides printed under the French translations should also give you confidence that you will be understood. If your listener should indicate that he doesn't understand, merely try again. A slight mispronunciation is no embarrassment.

Finally, to aid you in finding a phrase that you wish to use, the Dictionary has been partially indexed. The Dictionary itself is comprehensive enough so that you should not lack for words.

TIPS ON PRONUNCIATION AND ACCENT

The pronunciation of each word in this phrase book is indicated by a respelling that approximates the sounds of French, according to the following system:

The vowels:

a	Pronounced like "a" in c*a*t
ah	Pronounced like "a" in f*a*ther
eh	Pronounced like "e" in th*e*y
e	Pronounced like "e" in m*e*t
ee	Pronounced like "ee" in s*ee*n
eu	Pronounced like "ee" in s*ee*n but with pursed lips
o	Pronounced like "o" in b*o*y
oh	Pronounced like "o" in *o*ver
oo	Pronounced like "oo" in s*oo*n
uh	Pronounced like "a" in *a*way
oe	Pronounced like "u" in f*u*r
wah	Pronounced like "wa" in w*a*ter
ah-ee	Pronounced like "i" in *i*ce
y	Pronounced like "y" in *y*et

The consonants are sounded approximately as in English. In the pronunciation guides, the consonantal symbol "zh" sounds like the "s" in pleasure. The French "r" is pronounced far back in the throat and not, as in English, in the front of the mouth.

The French language uses what are known as "nasal vowels." In standard French writing, a nasal vowel is generally indicated by the placing of a single "n" or "m" after the vowel. To pronounce a nasal vowel, make the sound of English "ng" in si*ng*, but instead of bringing the back part of the tongue in contact with the back part of the throat, keep the tongue lax and push the air out through the nose. In this book a nasal vowel will be indicated in the pronunciation guide by the vowel in question followed by "ñ."

The accent in a French word is distributed fairly evenly over the syllables. However, in normal spoken French, there is a tendency to give a slightly stronger emphasis to the last syllable.

Salutations
and
Greetings

Even before you learn anything else in a foreign language,
you will want to learn how to greet people. Here are
some short expressions that you will find easy to learn and to
use when you meet people in a foreign land or along the
way, perhaps on the ship or the plane.

Good morning.
Bonjour.
Bohñ-zhoor.

Good day.
Bonjour.
Bohñ-zhoor.

Good afternoon.
Bonjour.
Bohñ-zhoor.

Good evening.
Bonsoir.
Bohñ-swahr.

Good-bye.
Adieu.
A-dyóē.

Good night.
Bonne nuit.
Bon nêû-ee.

How are you?
Comment allez-vous?
Ko-mahñ ta-leh voo?

Well, thank you. And you?
Bien, merci. Et vous?
Byañ mer-see. Eh voo?

How is Mr. . . . ?
Comment va Monsieur. . . ?
Ko-mahñ va muh-syôe. . . ?

How is Mrs. . . . ?
Comment va Madame. . . ?
Ko-mahñ va ma-dam . . . ?

Is Miss . . . well?
Est-ce que Mademoiselle . . . va bien?
Es kuh mad-mwah-zel . . . va byañ?

May I present my wife?
Puis-je présenter ma femme?
Péû-eezh preh-zahñ-teh ma fam?

This is my husband.
C'est mon mari.
Se mohñ ma-ree.

Pleased to meet you.
Enchanté (m) / Enchantée (f) de faire votre connaissance.
Ahñ-shahñ-teh / Ahñ-shahñ-teh duh fer votr ko-ne-sahñs.

This is my friend.
C'est mon ami (m).
Se mohñ nam-ee.

This is my friend.
C'est mon amie (f).
Se mohñ nam-ee.

This is my mother and my father.
C'est ma mère et mon père.
Se ma mer eh mohñ per.

This is my sister and my brother.
C'est ma soeur et mon frère.
Se ma sôer eh mohñ frer.

Is this your daughter?
Est-ce votre fille?
Es votr feey?

Is this your son?
Est-ce votre fils?
Es votr fees?

I hope that we will meet again.
J'espère que nous nous rencontrerons de nouveau.
Zhes-per kuh noo noo rahñ-kohñ-tre-rohñ duh noo-voh.

I'll see you tomorrow.
À demain.
A duh-mañ.

I'll be seeing you.
Au revoir.
Oh ruh-vwahr.

Excuse me.
Excusez-moi.
Ek-skéù-zeh mwah.

Pardon me.
Pardonnez-moi. / Pardon.
Par-don-eh mwah. / Par-dohñ.

I'm very sorry.
Je le regrette beaucoup.
Zhuh luh ruh-gret boh-koo.

Don't mention it.
Il n'y a pas de quoi.
Eel nee a pah duh kwah.

You're welcome.
Il n'y a pas de quoi. / De rien.
Eel nee a pah duh kwah. / Duh ree-yañ.

With pleasure.
Avec plaisir.
A-vek ple-zeer.

Please.
S'il vous plaît.
Seel voo ple.

Please . . .
Prière de . . .
Pree-yer duh . . .

Good luck!
Bonne chance!
Bon shahñs!

The Weather

The weather is one thing everyone has in common, and it is a universal topic of conversation. The phrases given here — combined with a bit of added vocabulary — are easily mastered, for they "pattern" in an understandable manner: "It's raining." "It's snowing."

It's nice weather today.
Il fait beau temps aujourd'hui.
Eel fe boh tahñ oh-zhoor-déû-ee.

It's bad weather today.
Il fait mauvais temps aujourd'hui.
Eel fe moh-ve tahñ oh-zhoor-déû-ee.

It's cold.
Il fait froid.
Eel fe frwah.

It's warm.
Il fait chaud.
Eel fe shoh.

Is it raining?
Pleut-il?
Plöe teel?

Yes, it's raining.
Oui, il pleut.
Wee, eel plöe.

No, it's not raining.
Non, il ne pleut pas.
Nohñ, eel nuh plöe pah.

It's snowing.
Il neige.
Eel nezh.

It rains (snows) here every day.
Il pleut (neige) ici tous les jours.
Eel plöe (nezh) ee-see too leh zhoor.

It's beginning to rain (to snow).
Il commence à pleuvoir (neiger).
Eel ko-mahñs a plöe-vwahr (ne-zheh).

It often rains (snows) here.
Il pleut (neige) souvent ici.
*Eel plöe (nezh) soo-vahñ
ee-see.*

It will rain (snow) tomorrow.
Il pleuvra (neigera) demain.
*Eel plöe-vra (ne-zhuh-ra)
duh-mañ.*

It rained (snowed) yesterday.
Hier il a plu (neigé).
Yer eel a plêu (ne-zheh).

It has stopped raining (snowing).
Il a cessé de pleuvoir (neiger).
Eel a se-seh duh plöe-vwahr (ne-zheh).

It's windy.
Il fait du vent.
Eel fe dêu vahñ.

There's a lot of fog.
Il y a beaucoup de brouillard.
Eel ee a boh-koo duh broo-ee-yar

The sun is rising.
Le soleil se lève.
Luh so-lehy suh lev.

The sun is setting.
Le soleil se couche.
Luh so-lehy suh koosh.

How is the weather?
Quel temps fait-il?
Kel tahñ fe teel?

I need an umbrella.
J'ai besoin d'un parapluie.
Zheh buh-zwañ dõeñ pa-ra-plêû-ee.

Will it be cool there?
Est-ce qu'il fera frais là?
Es keel fuh-ra fre la?

Will it be damp there?
Est-ce qu'il sera humide là?
Es keel suh-ra êû-meed la?

Should I take a sweater?
Devrais-je prendre un chandail?
Duh-vrezh prahñdr õeñ shahñ-dah-ee?

a raincoat?
un imperméable?
õeñ nañ-per-meh-abl?

a jacket?
une jaquette?
êûn zha-ket?

It's lightning.
Il fait des éclairs.
Eel fe deh zeh-kler.

It's thundering.
Il tonne.
Eel ton.

Cold weather.
Du temps froid.
Dêû tahñ frwah.

Warm weather.
Du temps chaud.
Dêû tahñ shoh.

Cold water.
De l'eau froide.
Duh loh frwahd.

Warm water.
De l'eau chaude.
Du loh shohd.

Hot water.
De l'eau très chaude.
Duh loh tre shohd.

I see . . .	**I'm afraid of . . .**	**I like . . .**
Je vois . . .	J'ai peur de . . .	J'aime . . .
Zhuh vwah . . .	*Zheh poer duh . . .*	*Zhem . . .*

the rain.
la pluie.
la pléû-ee.

the wind.
le vent.
luh vahñ.

the snow.
la neige.
la nezh.

the ice.
la glace.
la glas.

the sky.
le ciel.
luh syel.

the sun.
le soleil.
luh so-lehy.

the moon.
la lune.
la léûn.

the stars.
les étoiles.
leh zeh-twahl.

a star.
une étoile.
éûn eh-twahl.

a rainbow.
un arc-en-ciel.
óeñ nark ahñ syel.

a cloud.
un nuage.
óen néû-ahzh.

the clouds.
les nuages.
leh néû-ahzh.

the lightning.
les éclairs / la foudre.
leh zeh-kler / la foodr.

the thunder.
le tonnerre.
luh ton-er.

the storm.
l'orage.
lo-rahzh.

General Expressions

In this section you will find the most useful expressions — the ones you will use over and over again. They are the phrases that you should have on the tip of the tongue, ready for immediate use — particularly those that express desire or volition. Here they have been kept short for easy acquisition and speedy communication. You will see them appear again and again in other sections of this book, where they are used in particular situations.

What is your name?
Comment vous appelez-vous?
Ko-mahñ voo za-puh-leh voo?

My name is . . .
Je m'appelle . . .
Zhuh ma-pel . . .

What is his (her) name?
Comment s'appelle-t-il (elle)?
Ko-mahñ sa-pel teel (tel)?

I don't know.
Je ne sais pas.
Zhuh nuh se pah.

His (Her) name is . . .
Il (Elle) s'appelle . . .
Eel (El) sa-pel . . .

Do you know him (her)?
Le (La) connaissez-vous?
Luh (La) ko-ne-se voo?

Yes, I know him (her).
Oui, je le (la) connais.
Wee, zhuh luh (la) ko-ne.

No, I don't know him (her).
Non, je ne le (la) connais pas.
Nohñ, zhuh nuh luh (la) ko-ne pah.

I know you.
Je vous connais.
Zhuh voo ko-ne.

Where do you live?
Où demeurez-vous?
Oo duh-môè-reh voo?

I live here.
Je demeure ici.
Zhuh duh-môèr ee-see.

At what hotel are you staying?
À quel hôtel descendez-vous?
A kel oh-tel de-sahñ-deh voo?

She's a beautiful woman.
C'est une belle femme.
Se têun bel fam.

She's a pretty girl.
C'est une jolie jeune fille.
Se têun zho-lee zhôèn feey.

He's a handsome man.
C'est un bel homme.
Se tôèñ bel om.

I love you.
Je t'aime.
Zhuh tem.

I love her.
Je l'aime.
Zhuh lem.

I love him.
Je l'aime.
Zhuh lem.

Do you know where he lives?
Savez-vous où il demeure?
Sa-veh voo oo eel duh-môèr?

Do you speak English?
Parlez-vous anglais?
Par-leh voo ahñ-gle?

Please say it in English.
Dites-le en anglais, s'il vous plaît.
Deet-luh ahñ nahñ-gle, seel voo ple.

Is there anyone here who speaks English?
Y a-t-il ici quelqu'un qui parle anglais?
Ee a teel ee-see kel-kõeñ kee parl ahñ-gle?

Do you understand?
Comprenez-vous?
Kohñm-pruh-neh voo?

Yes, I understand.
Oui, je comprends.
Wee, zhuh kohñm-prahñ.

No, I don't understand.
Non, je ne comprends pas.
Nohñ, zhuh nuh kohñm-prahñ pah.

I understand a little.
Je comprends un peu.
Zhuh kohñm-prahñ õeñ põe.

I don't understand everything.
Je ne comprends pas tout.
Zhuh nuh kohñm-prahñ pah too.

Please speak more slowly.
Parlez plus lentement, s'il vous plaît.
Par-leh plõu lahñt-mahñ, seel voo ple.

Please repeat.
Répétez, s'il vous plaît.
Reh-peh-teh, seel voo ple.

What did you say?
Qu'est-ce que vous avez dit?
Kes kuh voo za-veh dee?

Bring me . . .
Apportez-moi . . .
A-por-teh mwah . . .

Tell me . . .
Dites-moi . . .
Deet mwah . . .

Give me . . .
Donnez-moi . . .
Do-neh mwah . . .

Show me . . .
Montrez-moi . . .
Moñ-treh mwah . . .

Send me . . .
Envoyez-moi . . .
Ahñ-vwah-yeh mwah. . .

Write to me . . .
Écrivez-moi . . .
Eh-kree-veh mwah . . .

I need . . .
J'ai besoin de . . .
Zheh buh-zwañ duh . . .

I would like . . .
Je voudrais . . .
Zhuh voo-dre . . .

I want . . .
Je veux . . .
Zhuh vŏe . . .

I don't want . . .
Je ne veux pas . . .
Zhuh nuh vŏe pah . . .

I can do that.
Je peux faire ça.
Zhuh pŏe fer sa.

I cannot do that.
Je ne peux pas faire ça.
Zhuh nuh`pŏe pah fer sa.

Have you . . . ?
Avez-vous . . . ?
A-veh voo . . . ?

Are you . . . ?
Êtes-vous . . . ?
Et voo . . . ?

Where is . . . ?
Où est . . . ?
Oo e . . . ?

Where are . . . ?
Où sont . . . ?
Oo soñ . . . ?

Where are you going?
Où allez-vous?
Oo a-leh voo?

Where is he going?
Où va-t-il?
Oo va teel?

Where are we going?
Où allons-nous?
Oo a-loñ noo?

I will wait here.
J'attendrai ici.
Zha-tahñ-dre ee-see.

How do you say that in French?
Comment dit-on cela en français?
Ko-mahñ dee-toñ suh-la ahñ frahñ-se?

What does that mean?
Qu'est-ce que cela signifie?
Kes kuh suh-la see-nyee-fee?

What do you mean?
Qu'est-ce que vous voulez dire?
Kes kuh voo voo-leh deer?

You are right (wrong).	**He is right (wrong).**
Vous avez raison (tort).	Il a raison (tort).
Voo zav-eh re-zoñ (tor).	*Eel a re-zoñ (tor).*

Without doubt.
San doute.
Sahñ doot.

How long must I wait?
Combien de temps dois-je attendre?
Kohñm-byañ duh tahñ dwahzh a-tahñdr?

Wait here until I come back.
Attendez ici jusqu'a ce que je revienne.
A-tahñ-deh ee-see jêûs-ka suh zhuh ruh-vyen.

Come here.	**Is it near here?**
Venez ici.	Est-ce que c'est près d'ici?
Vuh-neh ee-see.	*Es kuh se pre dee-see?*

Come in.	**Is it far from here?**
Entrez.	Est-ce que c'est loin d'ici?
Ahñ-treh.	*Es kuh se lwañ dee-see?*

It's possible.	**It's impossible.**
C'est possible.	C'est impossible.
Se po-seebl.	*Se tañm-po-seebl.*

Emergencies

You will probably never need to use any of the brief cries, entreaties, or commands that appear here, but accidents do happen, items may be mislaid or stolen, and mistakes do occur. If an emergency does arise, it will probably be covered by one of these expressions.

Help!
Au secours!
Oh suh-koor!

Help me!
Aidez-moi!
E-deh mwah!

There has been an accident!
Il y a eu un accident!
Eel ee a éü ŏeñ nak-see-dahñ!

Stop!
Arrêtez-vous!
A-re-teh voo!

Hurry up!
Dépêchez-vous!
Deh-pe-sheh voo!

Look out!
Attention!
A-tahñ-syoñ!

Send for a doctor!
Faites venir un médecin!
Fet vuh-neer ðeñ meh-duh-sañ!

Poison!
Poison!
Pwah-zoñ!

Fire!
Au feu!
Oh föe!

Police!
Police!
Po-lees!

What happened?
Qu'est-ce qui est arrivé?
Kes kee e ta-ree-veh?

What's the matter?
Qu'y a-t-il?
Kee a teel?

Don't worry!
Ne vous inquiétez pas!
Nuh voo zañ-kyeh-teh pah!

I missed the train (bus, plane).
J'ai manqué le train (l'autobus, l'avion).
Zheh mahñ-keh luh trañ (loh-toh-bêûs, la-vyon).

I've been robbed!
On m'a volé!
Oñ ma vo-leh!

That man stole my money!
Cet homme m'a volé l'argent!
Set om ma vo-leh lar-zhahñ!

Call the police!
Appelez la police!
A-puh-leh la po-lees!

I have lost my money!
J'ai perdu mon argent!
Zheh per-dêû moñ nar-zhahñ!

I have lost my passport!
J'ai perdu mon passeport!
Zheh per-dêû moñ pas-por!

It's an American (British) passport.
C'est un passeport américain (anglais).
Se tóèñ pas-por a-meh-ree-kañ (ahñ-gle).

Stay where you are!
Restez où vous êtes!
Res-teh oo voo zet!

Don't move!
Ne bougez pas!
Nuh boo-zheh pah!

Signs and Notices

You could probably get along in a foreign land without speaking a word if only you could read the signs and notices that are posted and displayed as directions and advertising. A sign is an immediate communication to him who can read it, and the pronunciation doesn't matter. To help you in some usual situations, here are the common signs. Some of them will help you avoid embarrassment, and others danger. And some of them will make life more pleasant.

À DROITE, To the right
À GAUCHE, To the left
ALLEZ, Go
ARRÊT, Stop
ATTENDEZ, Wait
AVERTISSEUR D'INCENDIE, Fire alarm
AVIS, Warning
CABINES, Lavatory

CABINET DE TOILETTES, Toilet
CAISSIER, Cashier
C'EST DANGEREUX, It's dangerous
CHAMBRES MEUBLÉES À LOUER,
  Furnished rooms to let
CHAUD, Warm
CHEMIN ÉTROIT, Narrow road
COLLINE, Hill
CONDUISEZ LENTEMENT, Go slow
COURBE, Curve
CROISEMENT DANGEREUX, Dangerous crossroad
CROISEMENT DE CHEMIN DE FER,
  Railroad crossing
DAMES, Women
DANGER, Danger
DÉFENDU, Forbidden
DÉFENSE DE FUMER, No smoking
DÉFENSE D'ENTRER, No admittance
DÉFENSE DE STATIONNER, No parking
DÉVIATION, Detour
ÉCOLE, School
ÉGLISE, Church
ENTRÉE, Entrance
ENTRÉE LIBRE, Admission free
ESSUIE-MAINS, Hand towels
FEMMES, Women
FERMÉ, Closed
FROID, Cold
HOMMES, Men
IL EST PERMIS DE FUMER, Smoking permitted
LENTEMENT, Slow
LIBRE, Free

MESSIEURS, Men
NE BUVEZ PAS L'EAU, Do not drink the water
N'ENTREZ PAS ICI, Keep out
NE TOUCHEZ PAS, Do not touch
OCCUPÉ, Occupied
OUVERT, Open
PAS DE VIRAGE À DROITE, No right turn
PAS DE VIRAGE À GAUCHE, No left turn
PÉAGE, Toll
PONT ÉTROIT, Narrow bridge
POUSSEZ, Push
PRÉCAUTION, Caution
PRIÈRE DE NE PAS TOUCHER, Do not touch
RELENTISSEZ, Slow
RENSEIGNEMENTS, Information
RUE BARRÉE, No thoroughfare
SALLE À MANGER, Dining room
SALLE D'ATTENTE, Waiting room
SALLE DE BAIN, Bathroom
SENS UNIQUE, One way
SONNEZ, Ring
SORTIE, Exit
STATIONNEMENT, Parking
TENEZ LA DROITE, Keep to the right
TIREZ, Pull
TOILETTE, Lavatory
TOURNANT DANGEREUX, Dangerous curve
TRAVAUX, Men at work
VIRAGE, Curve

Numbers, Time and Dates

You may only want to count your change or make an appointment or catch a train, but you will need to know the essentials of counting and telling time if you wish to stay on schedule, buy gifts, or pay for accommodations. In Europe, you should remember, time is often told by a twenty-four hour system. Thus 10 P.M. is described as 2200 and 10:30 P.M. as 2230.

Cardinal Numbers

one	**two**
un, une	deux
бeñ, êun	*dбè*
three	**four**
trois	quatre
trwah	*katr*
five	**six**
cinq	six
sañk	*seess*

seven
sept
set

eight
huit
êù-eet

nine
neuf
nöef

ten
dix
deess

eleven
onze
oñz

twelve
douze
dooz

thirteen
treize
trez

fourteen
quatorze
ka-torz

fifteen
quinze
kañz

sixteen
seize
sez

seventeen
dix-sept
deess-set

eighteen
dix-huit
deez-êù-eet

nineteen
dix-neuf
deez-nöef

twenty
vingt
vañ

twenty-one
vingt et un
vañ teh öeñ

twenty-two
vingt-deux
vañt-döe

thirty
trente
trahñt

thirty-one
trente et un
trahñt eh öeñ

forty
quarante
ka-rahñt

fifty
cinquante
sañ-kahñt

sixty
soixante
swah-ssahñt

seventy
soixante-dix
swah-ssahñt deess

eighty
quatre-vingts
katr vañ

ninety
quatre-vingt-dix
katr vañ deess

one hundred
cent
sahñ

two hundred
deux cents
dōe sahñ

three hundred
trois cents
trwah sahñ

five hundred
cinq cents
sañ sahñ

one thousand
mille
meel

one million
un million
ōeñ mee-lyoñ

nineteen hundred seventy- . . .
mille neuf cents soixante-dix . . .
meel nōef sahñ swah-ssahñt deess . . .

one man
un homme
ōeñ nom

one woman
une femme
eûn fam

one child
un enfant
ōeñ nahñ-fahñ

two men
deux hommes
dōe zom

two women
deux femmes
dōe fam

two children
deux enfants
dōe zahñ-fahñ

Some Ordinal Numbers

the first
le premier
luh pruh-myeh

the second
le deuxième
luh dŏē-zyehm

the third
le troisième
luh trwah-zyem

the fourth
le quatrième
luh ka-tree-yem

the fifth
le cinquième
luh sañ-kyem

the sixth
le sixième
luh see-zyem

the seventh
le septième
luh se-tyem

the eighth
le huitième
luh ĕù-ee-tyem

the ninth
le neuvième
luh nŏē-vyem

the tenth
le dixième
luh dee-zyem

the first man
le premier homme
luh pruh-myer om

the first woman
la première femme
la pruh-myer fam

the first child
le premier enfant
luh pruh-myer ahñ-fahñ

the fifth floor
le cinquième étage
luh sañ-kyem eh-tahzh

the third day
le troisième jour
luh trwah-zyem zhoor

the fourth street
la quatrième rue
la ka-tree-yem rēù

the second building
le deuxième édifice
luh dŏē-zyem eh-dee-feess

Telling Time

What time is it?
Quelle heure est-il?
Kel ŏer e teel?

It's one o'clock.
Il est une heure.
Eel e téûn ŏer.

It's two o'clock.
Il est deux heures.
Eel e dŏe zŏer.

It's a quarter after two.
Il est deux heures et quart.
Eel e dŏe zŏer eh kar.

It's half past two.
Il est deux heures et demie.
Eel e dŏe zŏe eh duh-mee.

It's a quarter till two.
Il est deux heures moins le quart.
Eel e dŏe zŏer mwañ luh kar.

It's ten after two.
Il est deux heures dix.
Eel e dŏe zŏer deess.

It's ten till two.
Il est deux heures moins dix.
Eel e dŏe zŏer mwañ deess.

It's five o'clock.
Il est cinq heures.
Eel e sañk ŏer.

It's ten o'clock.
Il est dix heures.
Eel e deez ŏer.

It's noon.
Il est midi.
Eel e mee-dee.

It's midnight.
El est minuit.
Eel e mee-nêû-ee.

It's early.
Il est tôt.
Eel e toh.

It's late.
Il est tard.
Eel e tahr.

one second
une seconde
éun suh-koñd

five seconds
cinq secondes
sañ suh-koñd

one minute
une minute
éun mee-néut

five minutes
cinq minutes
sañ mee-néut

one quarter hour
un quart d'heure
óen kar dóer

one half hour
une demie heure
éun duh-mee óer

one hour
une heure
éun óer

five hours
cinq heures
sañk óer

At what time are you leaving?
À quelle heure partez-vous?
A kel óer par-teh voo?

When do you arrive?
Quand arrivez-vous?
Kahñ ta-ree-veh voo?

When will we arrive?
Quand arriverons-nous?
Kahñ ta-ree-vuh-rohñ noo?

When shall we meet?
Quand est-ce que nous nous rencontrerons?
Kahñ ess-kuh noo noo rahñ-kohñ-truh-rohñ?

Meet me here at five o'clock.
Rencontrez-moi ici à cinq heures.
Rahñ-kohñ-treh-mwah ee-see a sank óer.

At what time do you get up?
À quelle heure vous levez-vous?
A kel óer voo luh-veh voo?

At what time do you go to bed?
À quelle heure vous couchez-vous?
A kel óer voo koo-sheh voo?

Dates

today
aujourd'hui
oh-zhoor-déû-ee

tomorrow
demain
duh-mañ

yesterday
hier
yer

one day
un jour
6en zhoor

two days
deux jours
dôe zhoor

five days
cinq jours
sañ zhoor

the day after tomorrow
après-demain
a-pre duh-mañ

the day before yesterday
avant-hier
a-vahñt yer

the morning
le matin
luh ma-tañ

the afternoon
l'après-midi
la-pre mee-dee

the evening
le soir
luh swar

the night
la nuit
la néû-ee

the week
la semaine
la suh-men

the month
le mois
luh mwah

the year
l'an / l'année
lahñ / lan-eh

last week
la semaine dernière / la semaine passé
la suh-men der-nyer / pa-seh

last month
le mois dernier / le mois passé
luh mwah der-nyeh / pa-seh

last year
l'année dernière / l'année passée
lah-neh der-nyer / pa-seh

this week
cette semaine
set suh-men

this month
ce mois
suh mwah

this year
cette année
set an-eh

next week
la semaine prochaine
la suh-men pro-shen

next month
le mois prochain
luh mwah pro-shañ

next year
l'année prochaine
lan-eh pro-shen

this morning
ce matin
suh ma-tañ

yesterday morning
hier matin
yer ma-tañ

tomorrow morning
demain matin
duh-mañ ma-tañ

this evening
ce soir
suh swar

yesterday evening
hier soir
yer swar

tomorrow evening
demain soir
dah-mañ swar

every day
tous les jours / chaque jour
too leh zhoor / shak zhoor

two days ago
il y a deux jours
eel ee a dœ̄e zhoor

The Days of the Week

Monday
lundi
lŏèn-dee

Tuesday
mardi
mar-dee

Wednesday
mercredi
mer-kruh-dee

Thursday
jeudi
zhŏè-dee

Friday
vendredi
vahñ-druh-dee

Saturday
samedi
sam-dee

Sunday
dimanche
dee-mahñsh

The Months of the Year

January
janvier
zhahñ-vee-eh

February
février
feh-vree-eh

March
mars
marss

April
avril
a-vreel

May
mai
me

June
juin
zhêu-añ

July
juillet
zhêu-ee-yeh

August
août
oot

September
septembre
sep-tahñmbr

October
octobre
ok-tobr

November
novembre
no-vahñmbr

December
décembre
deh-sahñmbr

The Seasons

the spring
le printemps
luh prañ-tahñ

the summer
l'été
leh-teh

the autumn
l'automne
loh-ton

the winter
l'hiver
lee-ver

Changing Money

Whether poet or businessman, you will need cash as you travel. Sooner or later, every traveler meets the problem of how to manage the exchange. The following phrases cover most situations you will encounter. You will help yourself if you obtain the latest official exchange rate before you leave home, and it can do no harm if you familiarize yourself with the sizes, shapes, and even colors of the various coins and bills. It is wise, too, to take along a small amount of the foreign currency for immediate use on your arrival.

Where is the nearest bank?
Où est la banque la plus proche?
Oo e la bahñk la pleü prosh?

Please write the address.
Écrivez l'adresse, s'il vous plaît.
Eh-kree-veh la-dress, seel voo ple.

I would like to cash this check.
Je voudrais toucher ce chèque.
Zhuh voo-dre too-sheh suh shek.

Will you cash this check?
Me changerez-vous ce chèque?
Muh shahñ-zhuh-reh voo suh shek?

Do you accept travelers' checks?
Acceptez-vous les chèques de voyageurs?
Ak-sep-teh voo leh shek duh vwah-ya-zhoͤer?

I want to change some money.
Je veux changer de l'argent.
Zhuh voͤ shahñ-zheh duh lar-zhahñ.

What kind?
Quelle espèce?
Kel es-pess?

Dollars.	**Pounds.**
Des dollars.	Des livres.
Deh do-lar.	*Deh leevr.*

What is the rate of exchange for the dollar (pound)?
Quel est le cours du dollar (de la livre)?
Kel e luh koor doͤu do-lar (duh la leevr)?

Your passport, please.
Votre passeport, s'il vous plaît.
Votr pas-por, seel voo ple.

How much do you wish to change?
Combien en désirez-vous changer?
Kohñm-byañ ahñ deh-zee-reh voo shahñ-zheh?

I want to change ten dollars.
Je veux changer dix dollars.
Zhuh voͤ shahñ-zheh dee do-lar.

Go to that clerk's window.
Allez au guichet de cet employé-là.
A-leh oh gee-sheh duh set ahñm-plwah-yeh la.

Here's the money.
Voici l'argent.
Vwah-see lar-shahñ.

Please give me some small change.
Donnez-moi de la petite monnaie, s'il vous plaît.
Do-neh mwah duh la puh-teet mo-ne, seel voo ple.

Here's your change.
Voici votre monnaie.
Vwah-see votr mo-ne.

Please count to see if it's right.
Comptez, s'il vous plaît, pour voir si c'est correct.
Kohñ-teh, seel voo ple, poor vwar see se ko-rekt.

Please sign this receipt.
Signez ce reçu, s'il vous plaît.
See-nyeh suh ruh-sêu, seel voo ple.

Can I change money here at the hotel?
Puis-je changer de l'argent ici à l'hôtel?
Pêu-eezh shahñ-zheh duh lar-zhahñ ee-see a loh-tel?

I'm expecting some money by mail.
J'attends de l'argent par la poste.
Zha-tahñ duh lar-zhahñ par la post.

Customs

Your first experience with French may be with the personnel or fellow passengers on a ship or a plane, but you will really begin to use the language when you come to customs. Here are some phrases that will speed your entry into the country and get you on your way again.

Have you anything to declare?
Avez-vous quelque chose à déclarer?
A-veh voo kel-kuh shoz a deh-kla-reh?

I have nothing to declare.
Je n'ai rien à déclarer.
Zhuh neh ree-yañ a deh-kla-reh.

Your passport, please.
Votre passeport, s'il vous plaît.
Votr pass-por, seel voo ple.

Here is my passport.
Voici mon passeport.
Vwah-see moñ pass-por.

Are these your bags?
Est-ce que celles-ci sont vos valises?
Es kuh sel see soñ voh va-leez?

Yes, and here are the keys.
Oui, et voici les clés.
Wee, eh vwah-see leh cleh.

Open this box.
Ouvrez cette boîte.
Oov-reh set bwaht.

Have you any cigarettes or tobacco?
Avez-vous des cigarettes ou du tabac?
A-veh voo deh see-ga-ret oo deû ta-ba?

I have only some cigarettes.
Je n'ai que des cigarettes.
Zhuh neh kuh deh see-ga-ret.

Close your bags.
Fermez vos valises.
Fer-meh voh va-leez.

You must pay duty.
Vous devez payer les droits de douane.
Voo duh-veh peh-yeh leh drwah duh doo-an.

They are for my personal use.
Ce sont pour mon usage personnel.
Suh soñ poor moñ neû-zahzh per-sso-nel.

How much must I pay?
Combien dois-je payer?
Kohñm-byañ dwahzh peh-yeh?

You must pay . . .
Vous devez payer . . .
Voo duh-veh peh-yeh . . .

May I go now?
Puis-je aller maintenant?
Péû-eezh a-leh mañt-nahñ?

Is that all?
Est-ce tout?
Ess too?

Porter, please carry this luggage.
Facteur, portez ces bagages, s'il vous plaît.
Fak-tôèr, por-teh seh ba-gazh, seel voo ple.

At the Hotel

Your accommodations may be a deluxe hotel, a modest hotel, a pension, or whatever, but it is important to be able to express your needs to be sure you get what you want. Outside of the cities, of course, few people are likely to be able to help you if you do not speak French, so we have given you the most useful expressions to cover most situations. They may make the difference between getting the room you want and having to settle for something less.

Which is the best hotel?
Quel est le meilleur hôtel?
Kel e luh meh-yœ̃r oh-tel?

This is a good hotel?
C'est un bon hôtel.
Se tõẽñ boñ noh-tel.

I like this hotel.
J'aime bien cet hôtel.
Zhem byañ set oh-tel.

I would like to take a room here.
Je voudrais prendre une chambre ici.
Zhuh voo-dre prahñdr ɛ̃un shahñmbr ee-see.

A single (double) room.
Une chambre à un lit (à deux lits).
Eun shahñmbr a öeñ lee (a döè lee).

A room with (without) bath.
Une chambre avec (sans) bain.
Eun shahñmbr a-vek (sahñ) bañ.

Is there a shower?
Y a-t-il une douche?
Ee a teel eun doosh?

May I see the room?
Puis-je voir la chambre?
Peu-eezh vwar la shahñmbr?

This is a large room.
C'est une grande chambre.
Se teun grahñd shahñmbr.

This room is too small.
Cette chambre est trop petite.
Set shahñmbr e tro puh-teet.

This room faces the street.
Cette chambre donne sur la rue.
Set shahñmbr don seur la reu.

Do you have a quieter room?
Avez-vous une chambre plus silencieuse?
A-veh voo eun shahñmbr pleu see-lahñ-syöez?

Do you have a room with a view of the ocean (court)?
Avez-vous une chambre avec une vue sur l'océan (la cour)?
A-veh voo eun shahñmbr a-vek eun veu seur loh-seh-ahñ (la koor)?

What is the price of this room?
Quel est le prix de cette chambre?
Kel e luh pree duh set shahñmbr?

That's much too expensive.
C'est beaucoup trop cher.
Se boh-koo tro sher.

That's very good.
C'est très bon.
Se tre boñ.

Does the price include breakfast?
Est-ce que le petit déjeuner est compris dans le prix?
Es kuh luh puh-tee deh-zhôe-neh e kohñm-pree dahñ luh pree?

Do you have a restaurant in the hotel?
Y a-t-il un restaurant dans l'hôtel?
Ee a-teel ôeñ re-stoh-rahñ dahñ loh-tel?

Must we eat our meals in the hotel restaurant?
Faut-il manger nos repas dans le restaurant de l'hôtel?
Foh-teel mahñ-sheh noh ruh-pah dahñ luh re-stoh-rahñ duh loh-tel?

Where is the dining room?
Où est la salle à manger?
Oo e la sal a mahñ-zheh?

We will stay here.
Nous resterons ici.
Noo res-te-rohñ ee-see.

How long will you stay?
Combien de temps resterez-vous?
Kohñm-byañ duh tahñ res-te-reh voo?

I will stay three weeks.
Je resterai trois semaines.
Zhuh res-te-re trwah suh-men.

We will stay three weeks.
Nous resterons trois semaines.
Noo res-te-roñ trwah suh-men.

Please fill out this card.
Remplissez cette carte, s'il vous plaît.
Rahñm-plee-seh set kart, seel voo ple.

My key, please.
Ma clé, s'il vous plaît.
Ma cleh, seel voo ple.

What number, sir?
Quel numéro, monsieur?
Kel néû-meh-ro, muh-syôè?

I have lost my key.
J'ai perdu ma clé.
Zheh per-déû ma cleh.

Where is the key to my room?
Où est la clé de ma chambre?
Oo e la cleh duh ma shahñmbr?

Where is the elevator?
Où est l'ascenseur?
Oo e la-ssahñ-ssôer?

Take my suitcase to my room.
Faites monter ma valise à ma chambre.
Fet moñ-teh ma va-leez a ma shahñmbr.

Where is the bathroom?
Où est la salle de bain?
Oo e la sal duh bañ?

Open the window, please.
Ouvrez la fenêtre, s'il vous plaît.
Oo-vreh la fuh-netr, seel voo ple.

Close the window, please.
Fermez la fenêtre, s'il vous plaît.
Fer-meh la fuh-netr, seel voo ple.

Please call the chambermaid.
Appelez la femme de chambre, s'il vous plaît.
A-pleh la fam de shahñmbr, seel voo ple.

I want to have these shirts washed.
Je veux faire laver ces chemises.
Zhuh vôè fer la-veh seh shuh-meez.

This is not my handkerchief.
Ce n'est pas mon mouchoir.
Suh ne pah moñ moo-shwar.

I want a towel and some soap.
Je veux un essuie-mains et du savon.
Zhuh vŏè zŏeñ ne-ssêû-ee mañ et dêû sa-voñ.

I want a clean towel.
Je veux un essuie-mains propre.
Zhuh vŏè ŏeñ ne-ssêû-ee mañ propr.

Please wake me at seven o'clock.
Éveillez-moi à sept heures, s'il vous plaît.
Eh-veh-yeh mwah a set ŏer, seel voo ple.

We are leaving tomorrow.
Nous partons demain.
Noo par-toñ duh-mañ.

Take my luggage down.
Faites descendre mes bagages.
Fet de-sahñdr meh ba-gazh.

Are there any letters for me?
Y a-t-il des lettres pour moi?
Ee a teel deh letr poor mwah?

I need some postage stamps.
J'ai besoin de quelques timbres-poste.
Zheh buh-zwañ duh kel-kuh tañmbr post.

Using the Telephone

Most visitors to foreign lands are wary of using the telephone when they should not be. Of course, gesturing and pointing are of no avail when you cannot see the person to whom you are speaking and have to depend entirely on what you hear and say. Still, it is possible to communicate if you make an effort. If there is difficulty, remember to ask the other person to speak slowly. It's your best assurance that the message will get through.

Where is there a telephone?
Où y a-t-il un téléphone?
Oo ee a teel бeñ teh-leh-fon?

I would like to telephone.
Je voudrais téléphoner.
Zhuh voo-dre teh-leh-fon-eh.

I would like to make a local (a long-distance) call to . . .
Je voudrais faire un coup de téléphone urbain (interurbain) à . . .
Zhuh voo-dre fer бeñ koo duh teh-leh-fon бûr-bañ (añ-ter-бûr-bañ) a . . .

What is the telephone number?
Quel est le numéro téléphonique?
Kel e luh néû-meh-ro teh-leh-fon-eek?

Where is the telephone book?
Où est l'annuaire du téléphone?
Oo e la-néû-er déû teh-leh-fon?

My number is . . .
Mon numéro est . . .
Moñ néû-meh-ro e . . .

I want number . . .
Je désire le numéro . . .
Zhuh deh-zeer luh néû-meh-ro . . .

Operator!
Téléphoniste!
Teh-leh-fon-eest!

Can I dial this number?
Puis-je composer ce numéro?
Péû-eezh kohñm-po-zeh suh néû-meh-ro?

How much is a telephone call to . . . ?
Combien coûte un coup de téléphone à . . . ?
Kohñm-byañ koot бeñ koo duh teh-leh-fon a . . . ?

I am ringing.
Je suis en train de sonner.
Zhuh séû-ee zahñ trañ duh so-neh.

Please do not hang up.
Ne quittez pas l'appareil, s'il vous plaît.
Nuh kee-teh pah la-pa-reh, seel voo ple.

Deposit coins.
Déposez des pièces de monnaie.
Deh-po-zeh deh pyess duh mo-neh.

They do not answer.
Ils ne répondent pas.
Eel nuh reh-poñd pah.

Please dial again.
Composez le numéro de nouveau, s'il vous plaît.
Kohñm-po-zeh luh néû-meh-ro duh noo-voh, seel voo ple.

The line is busy.
La ligne est occupée.
La leeny e to-kéû-peh.

Who is speaking?
Qui parle?
Kee parl?

May I speak to...?
Puis-je parler à...?
Péû-eezh parl-eh a...?

He (She) is not in.
Il (Elle) n'est pas ici.
Eel (el) ne pah ee-see.

Please speak more slowly.
Parlez plus lentement, s'il vous plaît.
Par-leh pléû lahñt-mahñ, seel voo ple.

Getting Around by Taxi and Bus

The drivers of taxis and buses almost never speak English, which may be fortunate when you relish a few peaceful moments. However, you will have to tell them where you're going, or want to go, and for that we've provided some handy phrases.

Call a taxi, please.
Appelez un taxi, s'il vous plaît.
Ap-leh бeň tak-see, seel voo ple.

Put my luggage into the taxi.
Mettez mes bagages dans le taxi.
Me-teh meh ba-gazh dahñ luh tak-see.

Driver, are you free?
Chauffeur, êtes-vous libre?
Shoh-főer, et voo leebr?

Where do you wish to go?
Où désirez-vous aller?
Oo deh-see-reh voo za-leh?

Drive to the railroad station (airport).
Conduisez-moi à la gare (l'aéroport).
Koñ-déû-ee-zeh mwah a la gar (la-eh-ro-por).

How much is the ride from here to the hotel?
Combien coûte le trajet d'ici à l'hôtel?
Kohñm-byañ koot luh tra-zheh dee-see a loh-tel?

Stop here!
Arrêtez ici!
A-re-teh zee-see!

I want to get out here.
Je veux descendre ici.
Zhuh voe de-ssahñdr ee-see.

Wait until I come back.
Attendez jusqu'à ce que je revienne.
A-tahñ-deh zhéûs-ka suh kuh zhuh ruh-vyen.

Wait for me here.
Attendez-moi ici.
A-tahñ-deh mwah ee-see.

Drive a little farther.
Allez un peu plus loin.
A-leh ôeñ pôe pléû lwañ.

Please drive carefully.
Conduisez avec soin, s'il vous plaît.
Koñ-déû-ee-zeh a-vek swañ, seel voo ple.

Please drive slowly.
Conduisez lentement, s'il vous plaît.
Koñ-déû-ee-zeh lahñt-mahñ, seel voo ple.

Turn to the left (right) here.
Tournez à gauche (droite) ici.
Toor-neh a gohsh (drwaht) ee-see.

Drive straight ahead.
Allez tout droit.
A-leh too drwah.

How much is the fare?
Quel est le prix de la course?
Kel a luh pree duh la koorss?

Which bus goes downtown?
Quel autobus va au centre de la ville?
Kel oh-toh-béuss va oh sahñtr duh la veel?

Bus number . . .
L'autobus numéro . . .
Loh-toh-béuss néu-meh-ro . . .

Does the bus stop here?
Est-ce que l'autobus s'arrête ici?
Es kuh loh-toh-béuss sa-ret ee-see?

Please tell me when we arrive at . . . street.
Dites-moi, s'il vous plaît, quand nous arriverons à la
  rue . . .
Deet mwah, seel voo ple, kahñ noo za-ree-ve-roñ a la réu . . .

Which bus goes to . . .?
Quel autobus va à . . .?
Kel oh-toh-béuss va a . . .?

Get on the bus here.
Montez dans l'autobus ici.
Moñ-teh dahñ loh-toh-béuss ee-see.

Get off the bus here.
Descendez de l'autobus ici.
De-sahñ-deh duh loh-toh-béuss ee-see.

Does this bus go to the museum?
Cet autobus va-t-il au musée?
Set oh-toh-béuss va teel oh méu-zeh?

Where must I transfer?
Où dois-je transférer?
Oo dwahzh trahñs-feh-reh?

When does the last bus leave?
Quand part le dernier autobus?
Kahñ par luh der-nyeh oh-toh-beùss?

Eating and Drinking

Merely going abroad is thrill enough for some persons; for others the high points of a trip are likely to be the hours spent at the table. Getting to know and appreciate the national cuisine and learning how to order native dishes are extra thrills for many travelers. Here, along with the phrases that are necessary to order your meals, we have added a menu reader of the most typical dishes of the cuisine in the countries where French is spoken.

I'm hungry.
J'ai faim.
Zheh fañ.

Are you hungry?
Avez-vous faim?
A-veh voo fañ?

I'm thirsty.
J'ai soif.
Zheh swahf.

Are you thirsty?
Avez-vous soif?
A-veh voo swahf?

I'm not hungry.
Je n'ai pas faim.
Zhuh neh pah fañ.

I'm not thirsty.
Je n'ai pas soif.
Zhuh neh pah swahf.

Do you want to eat now?
Voulez-vous manger maintenant?
Voo-leh voo mahñ-zheh mañt-nahñ?

Let's eat now.
Mangeons maintenant.
Mahñ-zhoñ mañt-nahñ.

Where is there a good restaurant?
Où y a-t-il un bon restaurant?
Oo ee a teel ⊖en boñ res-toh-rahñ?

The meals.
Les repas.
Leh ruh-pah.

breakfast
le petit déjeuner
luh puh-tee deh-zh⊖ê-neh

lunch
le déjeuner
luh deh-zh⊖ê-neh

dinner
le dîner
luh dee-neh

supper
le souper
luh soo-peh

At what time is breakfast (lunch, dinner)?
À quelle heure le petit déjeuner (le déjeuner, le dîner) est-il
    servi?
*A kel ⊖er luh puh-tee deh-zh⊖ê-neh (luh deh-zh⊖ê-neh, luh
    dee-neh) e teel ser-vee?*

I want breakfast (lunch, dinner) in my room.
Je veux le petit déjeuner (le déjeuner, le dîner) dans ma
    chambre.
*Zhuh v⊖ê luh puh-tee deh-zh⊖ê-neh (luh deh-zh⊖ê-neh, luh
    dee-neh) dahñ ma shahñmbr.*

I would like . . .
Je voudrais . . .
Zhuh voo-dre . . .

eggs
des oeufs
deh zŏē

fried eggs
des oeufs sur le plat
deh zŏē sĕur luh plah

scrambled eggs
des oeufs brouillés
deh zŏē broo-ee-yeh

two soft-boiled eggs
deux oeufs à la coque
dŏē zŏē a la kok

a poached egg
un oeuf poché
ŏēñ nŏēf po-sheh

bacon
du lard
dĕu lar

bread and butter
du pain et du beurre
dĕu pañ eh dĕu bŏēr

black coffee
du café noir
dĕu ka-feh nwar

coffee with milk
du café au lait
dĕu ka-feh oh le

coffee without milk
du café sans lait
dĕu ka-feh sahñ le

milk
du lait
dĕu le

tea
du thé
dĕu teh

ham
du jambon
dĕu zhahñm-boñ

cold meat
de la viande froide
duh la vyahñd frwahd

rolls
des petits pains
deh puh-tee pañ

Breakfast is ready.
Le petit déjeuner est prêt.
Luh puh-tee deh-zh-ŏeneh e pre.

Dinner is being served.
Le dîner est servi.
Luh dee-neh e ser-vee.

A table for two, please.
Une table pour deux, s'il vous plaît.
Eun tabl poor dŏe, seel voo ple.

Where is the waitress?
Où est la serveuse?
Oo e la ser-vŏez?

Waiter (Waitress), the menu, please.
Garçon (Mademoiselle), le menu, s'il vous plaît.
Gar-ssoñ (mad-mwah-zel), luh muh-neû, seel voo ple.

Waiter, please bring an ashtray.
Garçon, apportez un cendrier, s'il vous plaît.
Gar-ssoñ, a-por-teh ŏen sahñ-dree-yeh, seel voo ple.

What do you recommend?
Qu'est-ce que vous recommandez?
Kes kuh voo ruh-ko-mahñ-deh?

Do you recommend . . . ?
Recommandez-vous . . . ?
Ruh-ko-mahñ-deh voo . . . ?

Bring me some coffee now, please.
Apportez-moi du café maintenant, s'il vous plaît.
A-por-teh mwah deû ka-feh mañt-nahñ, seel voo ple.

More butter, please.
Plus de beurre, s'il vous plaît.
Pleû duh bŏer, seel voo ple.

Bring some more sugar.
Apportez encore dù sucre.
A-por-teh ahñ-kor deû seûkr.

Bring me a glass of water, please.
Apportez-moi un verre d'eau, s'il vous plaît.
A-por-teh mwah ŏen ver doh, seel voo ple.

This coffee is cold.
Ce café est froid.
Suh ka-feh e frwah.

Do you take milk and sugar?
Prenez-vous du lait et du sucre?
Pruh-neh voo dŏu le eh dŏu ŏuskr?

No sugar, thank you.
Pas de sucre, je vous remercie.
Pah duh sŏukr, zhuh voo ruh-mer-see.

We eat only fruit for breakfast.
Nous ne mangeons que de fruits au petit déjeuner.
Noo nuh mahñ-zhoñ kuh duh frŏu-ee oh puh-teedeh- zhŏe-neh.

This butter is not fresh.
Ce beurre n'est pas frais.
Suh bŏer ne pah fre.

The Condiments

the salt	**the pepper**
le sel	le poivre
luh sel	*luh pwahvr*
the sugar	**the oil**
le sucre	l'huile
luh sŏukr	*lŏueel*
the vinegar	**the mustard**
le vinaigre	la moutarde
luh vee-negr	*la moo-tard*

This milk is warm.
Ce lait est chaud.
Suh le e shoh.

This milk is sour.
Ce lait est aigre.
Suh le e tegr.

I would like a glass of cold milk.
Je voudrais un verre de lait froid.
Zhuh voo-dre ōen ver duh le frwah.

Another cup of coffee?
Encore une tasse de café?
Ahñ-kor ēun tass duh ka-feh?

Another cup of tea?
Encore une tasse de thé?
Ahñ-kor ēun tass duh teh?

Do you want some more tea?
Voulez-vous encore du thé?
Voo-leh voo ahñ-kor dēu teh?

Nothing more, thank you.
Rien de plus, je vous remercie.
Ree-yañ duh plēu, zhuh voo ruh-mer-see.

Foods and Beverages

the fish
le poisson
luh pwah-ssoñ

fruit
les fruits
leh frēu-ee

the meat
la viande
la vyahñd

the soup
le potage / la soupe
luh po-tahzh / la soop

vegetables
les légumes
leh leh-gēum

the water
l'eau
loh

the wine
le vin
luh vañ

the beer
la bière
la byer

At what time are the meals in this hotel?
À quelle heure sert-on les repas dans cet hôtel?
A kel 6er ser toñ leh ruh-pah dahñ set oh-tel?

We dine at seven o'clock.
Nous dînons à sept heures.
Noo dee-noñ a set 6er.

Here they dine at eight o'clock.
Ici on dîne à huit heures.
Ee-see oñ deen a 6û-eet 6er.

Please reserve a table for us.
Réservez une table pour nous, s'il vous plaît.
Reh-zer-veh 6ûn tabl poor noo, seel voo ple.

Do you want soup?
Voulez-vous du potage (de la soupe)?
Voo-leh voo d6û po-tahzh (duh la soop)?

Bring me a fork (a knife, a spoon).
Apportez-moi une fourchette (un couteau, une cuillère).
A-por-teh mwah 6ûn foor-shet (6eñ koo-toh, 6ûn k6û-ee-yer).

the cheese le fromage *luh fro-mahzh*	**the bread** le pain *luh pañ*
the butter le beurre *luh b6er*	**the milk** le lait *luh le*
the jam la compote *la koñ-pot*	**the honey** le miel *luh myel*
the salad la salade *la sa-lad*	

This fork is dirty.
Cette fourchette est sale.
Set foor-shet e sal.

This spoon isn't clean.
Cette cuillère n'est pas propre.
Set kêu-ee-yer ne pah propr.

Please bring me a napkin.
Apportez-moi une serviette, s'il vous plaît.
A-por-teh mwah êun ser-vee-yet, seel voo ple.

I would like a glass of wine.
Je voudrais un verre de vin.
Zhuh voo-dre ɓeñ ver duh vañ.

A glass of red (white) wine.
Un verre de vin rouge (blanc).
Oeñ ver duh vañ roozh (blahñ).

The Setting

a spoon
une cuillère
êun kêu-ee-yer

a small spoon
une petite cuillère
êun puh-teet kêu-ee-yer

a knife
un couteau
ɓeñ koo-toh

a small knife
un petit couteau
ɓeñ puh-tee koo-toh

a fork
une fourchette
êun foor-shet

a small fork
une petite fourchette
êun puh-teet foor-shet

a plate
une assiette / un plat
êun a-ssyet / ɓeñ plah

a tray
un plateau
ɓeñ pla-toh

a napkin
une serviette
êun ser-vee-yet

A bottle of wine.
Une bouteille de vin.
Euñ boo-tehy duh vañ.

This wine is too warm.
Ce vin est trop chaud.
Suh vañ e tro shoh.

A half bottle.
Une demi-bouteille.
Eun duh-mee boo-tehy.

Please bring some ice.
Apportez-moi de la glace.
A-por-teh mwah duh la glass.

I didn't order this.
Je n'ai pas commandé ceci.
Zhuh neh pah ko-mahñ-deh suh-see.

A glass of beer.
Un verre de bière.
Oeñ ver duh byer.

A bottle of beer.
Une bouteille de bière.
Eun boo-tehy duh byer.

To your health!
À votre santé!
A votr sahñ-teh!

Enjoy your meal!
Bon appétit!
Boñ na-peh-tee!

This tablecloth is not clean.
Cette nappe n'est pas propre.
Set nap ne pah propr.

Do you eat fish?
Mangez-vous le poisson?
Mahñ-zheh voo luh pwah-ssoñ?

He doesn't eat meat.
Il ne mange pas de viande.
Eel nuh mahñzh pah duh vyahñd.

I don't eat dessert.
Je ne mange pas de dessert.
Zhuh nuh mahñzh pah duh de-sser.

He would like some ice cream.
Il voudrait de la glace.
Eel voo-dre duh la glass.

Waiter, the check, please.
Garçon, l'addition, s'il vous plaît.
Gar-ssoñ, la-dee-syoñ, seel voo ple.

How much do I owe you?
Combien vous dois-je?
Kohñm-byañ voo dwahzh?

Is the tip included?
Est-ce que le service est compris?
Es kuh luh ser-vees e kohñm-pree?

Where do I pay?
Où est-ce que je paie?
Oo es kuh zhuh pe?

At the cashier's booth.
À la caisse.
A la kess.

I have already paid.
J'ai déjà payé.
Zheh deh-zha peh-yeh.

Here is a tip.
Voici un pourboire.
Vwah-see ŏeñ poor-bwar.

I left the tip on the table.
J'ai laissé le pourboire sur la table.
Zheh le-sseh luh poor-bwar sêur la tabl.

There is a mistake in the bill.
Il y a une erreur dans l'addition.
Eel ee a êun e-rŏer dahñ la-dee-syoñ.

Menu
Reader

Les Potages (*Soupes*) Soups

Bouillabaisse (*boo-ee-ya-behss*) Highly seasoned thick fish soup. French speciality.

Consommé (*kohñ-so-meh*) Clear soup.

Potage à la reine (*po-tahzh a la rehn*) Cream of chicken soup.

Potage au vermicelle (*po-tahzh oh ver-mee-sehl*) Noodle soup.

Potage Saint-Germain (*po-tahzh sañ zher-mañ*) Pea soup.

Soupe à l'oignon (*soop a lo-nyohñ*) Onion soup.

Le Poisson et Le Coquillage Fish and Shellfish

Crevette (*kruh-veht*) Shrimp.

Escargots (*ehs-kar-goh*) Snails, served in the shell, generally as a stew. French speciality.

Friture (*free-tēur*) Small fried fish.

Homard (*o-mar*) Lobster.

Huîtres (*ēu-eetr*) Oysters.

Langouste (*lahñ-goost*) Lobster or crayfish.

Maquereau (*ma-kuh-roh*) Mackerel.

Saumon fumé (*sho-mohñ fēu-meh*) Smoked salmon.

Sole (*sohl*) Sole.

Turbot (*tuhr-boh*) Turbot (Gourmet European flatfish).

La Viande et Les Spécialités Meat and Specialties

Bifteck (*beef-tehk*) Steak.

  saignant (*seh-nyahñ*) Rare.

  bien cuit (*byañ kēu-ee*) Well done.

Boeuf (*bōēf*) Beef.

Canard (*ka-nar*) Duck.

Cervelles (*sehr-vehl*) Brains.

Châteaubriand (*shah-toh-bree-yahñ*) Filet steak.

Coq au vin (*kok oh vañ*) Chicken in wine sauce.

Côtelette d'agneau (*koht-leht da-nyoh*) Lamb chop.

Gigot ragoût de mouton (*zhee-goh ra-goo duh moo-tohñ*) Leg of mutton stew.

Jambon (*zhahñm-bohñ*) Ham.

Pâté de foie gras (*pah-teh duh fwah grah*) Spread or paste prepared from goose livers. French speciality.

Pattes de grenouilles (*paht duh gruh-noo-eey*) Frogs' legs. French speciality.

Pot-au-feu (*pot-oh-fōē*) Meat and vegetable stew. French speciality.

Poulet (*poo-leh*) Chicken.

Ris de veau (*ree duh voh*) Sweetbreads.

Rôti de veau (*roh-tee duh voh*) Roast veal.

Les Oeufs et Le Pain Eggs and Bread

Brioches (*bree-osh*) Fluffy, round breakfast rolls.
Croissants (*krwah-shañ*) Crescent-shaped breakfast rolls.
Oeufs brouillés (*ŏe broo-ee-yeh*) Scrambled eggs.
Oeufs à la coque (*ŏe a la kok*) Soft-boiled eggs.
Omelette (*om-leht*) Omelet.
Petit pain (*puh-tee pañ*) Roll.

Les Légumes et Les Salades Vegetables and Salads

Artichaut (*ahr-tee-shoh*) Artichoke.
Asperges (*as-pehrzh*) Asparagus.
Betterave (*beht-rahv*) Beet.
Carotte (*ka-rot*) Carrot.
Céleri (*seh-luh-ree*) Celery.
Champignons (*shahñm-pee-nyohñ*) Mushrooms.
Choufleur (*shoo-flerr*) Cauliflower.
Crudités (*krêu-dee-teh*) Vegetable salad.
Épinards (*eh-pee-nar*) Spinach.
Haricots verts (*a-ree-koh ver*) String beans.
Oignons (*oh-nyohñ*) Onions.
Petits pois (*puh-tee pwah*) Green peas.
Pomme de terre (*pom duh ter*) Potato.
Pommes frites (*pom freet*) French fried potatoes.
Riz (*ree*) Rice.
Salade de laitue (*sa-lad duh leh-têu*) Lettuce salad.
Salade niçoise (*sa-lad nee-swahz*) Greek salad.
Tomates (*toh-maht*) Tomatoes.

Les Fruits et Les Desserts Fruits and Desserts

Ananas (*a-na-nah*) Pineapple.
Banane (*ba-nan*) Banana.
Cerises (*suh-reez*) Cherries.
Compotes de fruits (*kohñm-pot duh frêu-ee*) Stewed fruits.
Confitures (*kohñ-fee-têur*) Jam.
Creme à la vanille (*krehm ala va-neey*) Vanilla ice cream.

Fraises (*frehz*) Strawberries.
Fromage (*fro-mahzh*) Cheese.
Gâteau (*gah-toh*) Cake.
Glace à la vanille (*glass a la va-neey*) Vanilla ice cream.
Macedoine de fruits (*ma-seh-dwahn duh frêû-ee*) Fruit salad.
Pamplemousse (*pahñm-pluh-mooss*) Grapefruit.
Petits fours (*puh-tee foor*) Tea cakes.
Pomme (*pom*) Apple.
Raisins (*reh-zañ*) Grapes.
Yaourt (*yah-oot*) Yogurt.

Les Boissons Beverages

Bière (*byer*) Beer.
Café (*ka-feh*) Coffee.
  au lait (*oh leh*) With milk.
Chocolat (*sho-ko-lah*) Chocolate.
Cidre (*seedr*) Cider.
Eau (*oh*) Water.
Eau minérale (*oh-mee-neh-ral*) Mineral water.
Jus d'orange (*zhêû do-rahñzh*) Orange juice.
Lait (*leh*) Milk.
Thé (*teh*) tea.
Vin blanc (*vañ blahñ*) White wine.
Vin rouge (*vañ roozh*) Red wine.
Xérès sec (*sheh-reh sehk*) Dry sherry.
Xérés sucré (*sheh-reh sêû-kreh*) Sweet sherry.

Shopping

Shopping abroad is always an adventure and frequently a delight. It's not only the varied merchandise that you may buy to take home as gifts, but the sheer pleasure of making yourself understood. It's important to know, and to be able to explain, exactly what it is that you want, since, obviously, you won't be able to trot downtown a week later to make an exchange. You'll discover, too, that sizes and weights are different; so we have included conversion tables here. Here are the typical questions you or the salesman might ask or the statements you may make during your shopping trips.

I would like to go shopping.
Je voudrais aller faire des achats.
Zhuh voo-dre za-leh fer deh za-shah.

At what time do the stores open?
À quelle heure ouvre-t-on les magasins?
A kel ŏèr oovr toñ leh ma-ga-zañ?

At what time do the stores close?
À quelle heure ferme-t-on les magasins?
A kel ŏèr ferm toñ leh ma-ga-zañ?

Where is there . . . ?
Où y a-t-il?
Oo ee a teel . . . ?

an antique shop.
une boutique d'antiquités.
ềun boo-teek dahñ-tee-kee-teh.

a candy store.
une boutique de confiseur.
ềun boo-teek duh koñ-fee-zốer.

a dressmaker.
une couturière.
ềun koo-tềur-ee-yer.

a drugstore.
une pharmacie.
ềun far-ma-see.

a grocery.
une épicerie.
ềun eh-pee-suh-ree.

a hat shop.
un chapelier.
ồeñ sha-puh-lee-yeh.

a perfumery.
une parfumerie.
ềun par-fều-muh-ree.

a photography shop.
un magasin de photographie.
ồeñ ma-ga-zañ duh fo-to-gra-fee.

a book store.
une librairie.
ềun lee-bre-ree.

a department store.
un grand magasin.
ồeñ grahñ ma-ga-zañ.

a druggist.
un pharmacien.
ồeñ far-ma-syañ.

a florist.
une fleuriste.
ềun flồer-eest.

a greengrocer.
un fruitier.
ồeñ frều-ee-tee-yeh.

a jewelry store.
une bijouterie.
ềun bee-zhoo-tuh-ree.

Where is there . . . ?
Où y a-t-il?
Oo ee a teel . . . ?

---

a shoe store.
un magasin de chaussures.
бeñ ma-ga-zañ duh shoh-sséûr.

a tobacconist.
un bureau de tabac.
бeñ béû-roh duh ta-ba.

a watchmaker.
un horloger.
бeñ nor-lo-zheh.

a tailor.
un tailleur.
бeñ tah-ee-yбer.

a toy store.
un magasin de jouets.
бeñ ma-ga-zañ duh zhoo-e.

May I help you?
Puis-je vous servir?
Péû-eezh voo ser-veer?

Will you help me, please?
Me servirez-vous, s'il vous plaît?
Muh ser-veer-eh voo, seel voo ple?

Are you being served?
Est-ce que l'on vous sert?
Es kuh loñ voo ser?

What do you wish?
Que désirez-vous?
Kuh deh-zee-reh voo?

Do you sell . . . ?
Vendez-vous . . . ?
Vahñ-deh voo . . . ?

Do you have . . . ?
Avez-vous . . . ?
A-veh voo . . . ?

I would like . . .
Je voudrais . . .
Zhuh voo-dre . . .

a brassiere
un soutien-gorge
ɓeñ soo-tyañ gorzh

a handkerchief
un mouchoir
ɓeñ moosh-war

panties
un caleçon
ɓeñ kal-ssoñ

shoes
des souliers
deh soo-lyeh

a skirt
une jupe
eûn zheúp

socks
des chaussettes
deh shoh-sset

a suit
un complet
ɓeñ kohñm-ple

a tie
une cravatte
eûn kra-vat

underwear
sous-vêtements
soo-vet-mahñ

gloves
des gants
deh gahñ

a hat
un chapeau
ɓeñ sha-poh

a shirt
une chemise
eûn shuh-meez

shorts
un short
ɓeñ short

a slip
un jupon
ɓeñ zheû-poñ

stockings
des bas
deh bah

a sweater
un chandail
ɓeñ shahñ-dah-ee

an undershirt
un gilet de dessous
ɓeñ zhee-leh duh duh-ssoo

I would like to buy . . .
Je voudrais acheter . . .
Zhuh voo-dre zash-teh . . .

a battery
une batterie
êun bat-ree

a camera
un appareil photographique
ôèn na-pa-rehy fo-to-gra-feek

film
une pellicule
êun pe-lee-kêul

flashbulbs
des ampoules photographiques
deh zahñm-pool fo-to-gra-feek

a pen
une plume
nêu plêum

a pencil
un crayon
ôèñ kre-yoñ

postcards
des cartes postales
deh kart pos-tal

stamps
des timbres-poste
deh tañmbr post

lotion
de la friction
duh la freek-syoñ

powder
de la poudre
duh la poodr

razor blades
des lames de rasoir
deh lam duh ra-zwar

shampoo
du shampooing
dêu shahñm-poo-eeng

shaving cream
du savon à raser
dêu sa-voñ a ra-zeh

soap
du savon
dêu sa-voñ

toothbrush
une brosse à dents
êun bross a dahñ

toothpaste
de la pâte dentifrice
duh la paht dahñ-tee-freess

Please show me some . . .
Montrez-moi des . . . s'il vous plaît.
Moñ-treh mwah deh . . . seel voo ple.

What size, please?
Quelle taille, s'il vous plaît?
Kel tah-ee, seel voo ple?

Try on these . . .
Essayez ces . . .
E-sseh-yeh seh . . .

How much does it cost?
Combien coûte-t-il?
Kohñm-byañ koo-tuh-teel?

How much do they cost?
Combien coûtent-ils?
Kohñm-byañ koo-tuh-teel?

That is too expensive.
C'est trop cher.
Se tro sher.

That is cheap.
C'est bon marché.
Se boñ mar-sheh.

I like this one.
Celui-ci me plaît. / J'aime celui-ci.
Suh-leû-ee see muh ple. / Zhem suh-leû-ee see.

---

cigar
un cigare
6eñ see-gar

cigarettes
des cigarettes
deh see-ga-ret

flint
un silex
6eñ see-leks

fluid
du liquide
deû lee-keed

lighter
un briquet
6eñ bree-keh

matches
des allumettes
deh za-leû-met

I will take this one.
Je prendrai celui-ci.
Zhuh prahñ-dre suh-leû-ee see.

I don't like this color.
Cette couleur ne me plaît pas. / Je n'aime pas cette
   couleur.
Set koo-leur nuh muh ple pas. / Zhuh nem pah set koo-leur.

I prefer it in . . .
Je le préfère en . . .
Zhuh luh preh-fer ahñ . . .

black	**blue**	**brown**
noir	bleu	brun / marron
nwar	*blôè*	*brôèn / ma-roñ*
gray	**green**	**red**
gris	vert	rouge
gree	*ver*	*roozh*
white	**yellow**	**dark**
blanc	jaune	foncé
blahñ	*zhohn*	*foñ-seh*
light		
clair		
kler		

Sale	**For Sale**
Vente	En Vente
Vahñt	*Ahñ vahñt*
Clearance Sale	
Solde	
Sold	

This dress is too short.
Cette robe est trop courte.
Set rob e tro koort.

This skirt is too long.
Cette jupe est trop longue.
Set zhéup e tro loñg.

I would like to see a white shirt.
Je voudrais voir une chemise blanche.
Zhuh voo-dre vwar êun shuh-meez blahñsh.

He would like to see some white shirts.
Il voudrait voir des chemises blanches.
Eel voo-dre vwar deh shuh-meez blahñsh.

The sleeves are too wide.
Les manches sont trop larges.
Leh mahñsh soñ tro larzh.

The sleeves are too narrow.
Les manches sont trop étroites.
Leh mahñsh soñ tro peh-trwaht.

I would like to see some shoes.
Je voudrais voir des souliers (chaussures).
Zhuh voo-dre vwar deh soo-lyeh (shoh-ssêur).

A pair of black (brown) shoes.
Une paire de souliers noirs (bruns).
Êun per duh soo-lyeh nwar (brôeñ).

Try this pair on.
Essayez cette paire-ci.
E-sse-yeh set per see.

They are too narrow.
Ils sont trop étroits.
Eel soñ tro peh-trwah.

They are too tight (loose, long, short).
Ils sont trop justes (amples, longs, courts).
Eel soñ tro zhêust (ahñmpl, loñ, koor).

They are not big enough.
Ils ne sont pas assez grands.
Eel nuh soñ pah za-sseh grahñ.

Do you sell cigarettes?
Vendez-vous des cigarettes?
Vahñ-deh voo deh see-ga-ret?

Do you have matches?
Avez-vous des allumettes?
A-veh voo deh za-lêu-met?

I want to buy needles, pins, and some thread.
Je veux acheter des aiguilles, des épingles et du fil.
Zhuh vôe zash-teh deh ze-gêu-eey deh zeh-pañgl eh dêu feel.

How many of them do you want?
Combien en voulez-vous?
Kohñm-byañ ahñ voo-leh voo?

Anything else?	**No, thank you. That's all.**
Quelque chose d'autre?	Non, merci. C'est tout.
Kel-kuh shoz dohtr?	*Noñ, mer-see. Se too.*

I'll take it (them) with me.
Je le (les) prendrai avec moi.
Zhuh luh (leh) prahñ-dre a-vek mwah.

Will you wrap it, please?
Voulez-vous l'envelopper, s'il vous plaît?
Voo-leh voo lahñ-vuh-lo-peh, seel voo ple?

Send it to the hotel.
Envoyez-le à l'hôtel.
Ahñ-vwah-yeh luh a loh-tel.

Pack it (them) for shipment to . . .
Emballez-le (-les) pour l'expédier à . . .
Ahñm-ba-leh-luh (-leh) poor lek-peh-dyeh a . . .

Here is the bill.
Voici la note.
Vwah-see la not.

I will pay cash.
Je payerai comptant.
Zhuh peh-yuh-re koñ-tahñ.

Is there a discount?
Y a-t-il une remise?
Ee a-teel Ᾱn ruh-meez?

CLOTHING SIZE CONVERSIONS: *Women*

Dresses, Suits and Coats

American:	8	10	12	14	16	18
British:	30	32	34	36	38	40
Continental:	36	38	40	42	44	46

Blouses and Sweaters

American:	32	34	36	38	40	42	44
British:	34	36	38	40	42	44	46
Continental:	40	42	44	46	48	50	52

Stockings

American and British:	8	8½	9	9½	10	10½	11
Continental:		35	36	37	38	39	40	41

Shoes

American:	5	5½	6	6½	7	7½	8	8½	9
British:	3½	4	4½	5	5½	6	6½	7	7½
Continental:	35	35	36	37	38	38	38½	39	40

Gloves

American, British and Continental sizes are the same

CLOTHING SIZE CONVERSIONS: *Men*

Suits, Sweaters and Overcoats

American and British:	34	36	38	40	42	44	46	48
Continental:	44	46	48	50	52	54	56	58

Shirts

American and British:	14	14½	15	15½	16	16½	17	17½
Continental:		36	37	38	39	40	41	42	43

Socks

American and British:	9½	10	10½	11	11½	12	12½
Continental:		39	40	41	42	43	44	45

Shoes

American:	7	7½	8	8½	9	9½	10	10½	11	11½
British:	6½	7	7½	8	8½	9	9½	10	10½	11
Continental:	39	40	41	42	43	43	44	44	45	45

Getting Around by Automobile

Since few attendants who work at garages and stations speak English, some ability in French will be very useful. You will need gasoline, of course, and probably some regular servicing. And should there be some problem with the car, a lot of time and energy will be saved if you can explain your needs.

I would like to hire a car.
Je voudrais louer une auto (voiture).
Zhuh voo-dre loo-eh ũn oh-toh (vwah-tẽur).

How much does a car cost per day?
Combien coûte une voiture par jour?
Kohñm-byañ koot ũn vwah-tẽur par zhoor?

How much per kilometer?
Combien par kilomètre?
Kohñm-byañ par kee-loh-metr?

Is gasoline expensive in this country?
L'essence est-elle chère dans ce pays?
Le-ssahñss e tel sher dahñ suh peh-ee?

Is there a deposit?
Faut-il verser un acompte?
Foh-teel ver-seh ɓeñ na-kohñt?

I would like a car with seatbelts and an outside mirror, please.
Je voudrais une auto avec des ceintures de place et un miroir extérieur, s'il vous plaît.
Zhuh voo-dre ɐun oh-toh a-vek deh sañ-tɐur duh plass eh ɓeñ meer-war eks-teh-ree-yóɓer, seel voo ple.

I will (will not) take the car out of the country.
Je prendrai (ne prendrai pas) l'auto hors du pays.
Zhuh prahñ-dre (nuh prahñ-dre pah) loh-toh or dɐu peh-ee.

I want to leave it in . . .
Je veux la laisser à . . .
Zhuh vóɓe la le-seh a . . .

How much is the insurance per day?
Combien coûte l'assurance par jour?
Kohñm-byan koot la-sɐu-rahñs par zhoor?

Here is the registration and the key.
Voici l'enregistrement et la clé.
Vwah-see lahñ-re-zheestr-mahñ eh la cleh.

Where is there a gas station?
Où y a-t-il une station de service?
Oo ee a teel ɐun sta-syon duh ser-veess?

a garage?
un garage?
ɓeñ ga-rahzh?

Fill it up.
Faites-le plein.
Fet luh plañ.

Premium.
Super.
Sêû-per.

Regular.
Ordinaire.
Or-dee-ner.

I want twenty liters of gasoline.
Je veux vingt litres d'essence.
Zhuh vôê vañ leetr de-ssahñss.

I also need some oil.
J'ai besoin de l'huile aussi.
Zheh buh-zwañ duh lêû-eel oh-see.

Please put in some water.
Mettez de l'eau, s'il vous plaît.
Me-teh duh loh, seel voo ple.

Wash the car please.
Lavez la voiture, s'il vous plaît.
La-veh la vwah-têûr, seel voo ple.

Please inspect the tires.
Inspectez les pneus, s'il vous plaît.
Añ-spehk-teh leh pnôê, seel voo ple.

Put in some air.
Mettez de l'air.
Me-teh duh ler.

Is there a mechanic here?
Y a-t-il un mécanicien ici?
Ee a teel ôêñ meh-ka-nee-syañ ee-see?

Can you fix a flat tire?
Pouvez-vous réparer un pneu crevé?
Poo-veh voo reh-pa-reh ôêñ pnôê kruh-veh?

How long will it take?
Combien de temps ça faudra?
Kohñm-byañ duh tahñ sa foh-dra?

Have you a road map?
Avez-vous une carte routière?
A-veh voo ēun kart roo-tyer?

Where does this road go to?
Où va cette route?
Oo va set root?

Is this the road to . . . ?
Est-ce la route à . . . ?
Es la root a . . . ?

Is the road good?
La route est-elle bonne? / Le chemin est-il bon?
La root e tel bon? / Luh shuh-mañ e teel boñ?

A narrow road.
Une route étroite.
Oen root eh-trwaht.

A wide road.
Une route large.
Ēun root larzh.

A narrow bridge.
Un pont étroit.
Oeñ poñ eh-trwah.

A bad road.
Une mauvaise route. / Un mauvais chemin.
Ēun moh-vez root. / Oeñ moh-ve shuh-mañ.

This road is slippery when it's wet.
Ce chemin est glissant lorsqu'il est mouillé.
Suh shuh-mañ e glee-ssahñ lors-keel e moo-ee-yeh.

Is there a speed limit here?
Y a-t-il une limite de vitesse ici?
Ee a teel ēun lee-meet duh vee-tess ee-see?

You were driving too fast.
Vous conduisiez trop vite.
Voo koñ-dēu-ee-zee-yeh tro veet.

You must pay the fine.
Il faut que vous payiez l'amende.
Eel foh kuh voo peh-yee-yeh la-mahñd.

May I leave the car here?
Puis-je laisser la voiture ici?
Péû-eezh le-sseh la vwah-téûr ee-see?

May I park here?
Puis-je stationner ici?
Péû-eezh sta-syon-eh ee-see?

Where is the nearest garage?
Où est le garage le plus proche?
Oo e luh ga-rahzh luh pléû prosh?

This car isn't running well.
Cette voiture ne marche pas bien.
Set vwah-téûr nuh marsh pah byañ.

I have a driver's license.
J'ai un permis de conduire.
Zheh bêñ per-mee duh koñ-déû-eer.

Please check . . .
Examinez . . . s'il vous plaît.
Eg-za-mee-neh . . . seel voo ple.

Can you fix it?
Pouvez-vous le réparer?
Poo-veh voo luh reh-pa-reh?

How long will it take?
Combien de temps ça faudra?
Kohñm-byañ duh tahñ sa foh-dra?

Your car is ready.
Votre voiture est prête.
Votr vwah-téûr e pret.

Drive carefully!
Conduisez avec soin!
Koñ-déû-ee-zeh a-vek swañ!

Please wipe the windshield.
Nettoyez le pare-brise, s'il vous plaît.
Ne-twah-yeh luh par-breez, seel voo ple.

I don't know what the matter is.
Je ne sais pas ce qu'il y a.
Zhuh nuh se pah suh keel ee a.

I think it's . . .	**Is it . . . ?**
Je crois que c'est . . .	Est-ce . . .?
Zhuh krwah kuh se . . .	*Es . . . ?*

the accelerator.	**the air filter.**
l'accélérateur.	le filtre d'air.
lak-seh-leh-ra-tōer.	*luh feeltr der.*
the battery.	**the brakes.**
la batterie.	les freins.
la ba-tree.	*leh frañ.*
the carburetor.	**the clutch.**
le carburateur.	l'embrayage.
luh car-bēu-ra-tōer.	*lahñm-breh-yazh.*
the lights.	**the motor.**
les phares.	le moteur.
leh far.	*luh mo-tōer.*
the spark plugs.	**the tires.**
les bougies.	les pneus.
leh boo-zhee.	*leh pnōè.*
the wheel.	**the wheels.**
la roue.	les roues.
la roo.	*leh roo.*
the front wheel.	**the back wheel.**
la roue avant.	la roue arrière.
la roo a-vahñ.	*la roo a-ree-yer.*

Priority road ahead

Some International Road Signs

 = RED

 = BLUE

 = BLACK

Stop

Dangerous curve

Right curve

Double curve

Intersection

Intersection with secondary road

Railroad crossing
with gates

Railroad crossing
without gates

Road work

Pedestrian
crossing

Children

Road narrows

Uneven road

Slippery road

Traffic circle
ahead

Danger

Closed to
all vehicles

No entry

No left turn

No U turn

Overtaking
prohibited

Speed limit

Customs

No parking

Direction to
be followed

Traffic circle

No parking

Getting Around by Train

The railroad is the most frequently used means of transportation by visitors abroad. Schedules and timetables are usually readily understandable — if they are visible — but otherwise, in arranging your travel by train, you will need to use some of these phrases.

The railroad station.
La gare.
La gar.

The train.
Le train.
Luh trañ.

Drive to the railroad station.
Allez à la gare.
A-leh a la gar.

I need a porter.
J'ai besoin d'un facteur.
Zheh buh-zwañ dōēn fak-tōēr.

Porter, here is my luggage.
Facteur, voici mes bagages.
Fak-tōer vwah-see meh ba-gazh.

These are my bags.
Ce sont mes valises.
Suh soñ meh va-leez.

Here are the baggage checks.
Voici les bulletins.
Vwah-see leh bēul-tañ.

Where is the ticket window?
Où est le guichet?
Oo e luh gee-sheh?

Have you a timetable?
Avez-vous un horaire?
A-veh voo zōeñ nor-er?

When does the train leave?
Quand part le train?
Kahñ par luh trañ?

From which platform?
De quel quai?
Duh kel ke?

I want to check this baggage.
Je veux faire enregistrer ces bagages.
Zhuh vōe fer ahñ-re-zhees-treh seh ba-gazh.

I must pick up a ticket.
Je dois prendre un billet.
Zhuh dwah prahñdr ōeñ bee-yeh.

I want a ticket to . . .
Je veux un billet à . . .
Zhuh vōe zōeñ bee-yeh a . . .

First class.
Première classe.
Pruh-myer klass.

Second class.
Deuxième classe.
Dōe-zyem klass.

One way.
Aller seulement.
A-leh sōel-mahñ.

Round trip.
Aller et retour.
A-leh eh ruh-tour.

Is there a dining car?
Y a-t-il un wagon-restaurant?
Eee a teel ŏeñ va-goñ res-toh-rahñ?

Does this train go to . . .?
Est-ce que ce train va à . . . ?
Es kuh suh trañ va a . . . ?

Does this train stop at . . .?
Est-ce que ce train s'arrête à . . . ?
Es kuh suh trañ sa-ret a . . . ?

Is the train late?
Est-ce que le train est en retard?
Es kuh luh trañ e tahñ ruh-tar?

Is this seat occupied?
Est-ce que cette place est occupée?
Es kuh set plass e to-kêû-peh?

What is the name of this station?
Comment s'appelle cette gare?
Ko-mahñ sa-pel set gar?

How long do we stop here?
Combien de temps nous y arrêtons-nous?
Kohñm-byañ duh tahñ noo zee a-re-toñ noo?

May I open the window?
Puis-je ouvrir la fenêtre?
Pêû-eezh oo-vreer la fuh-netr?

Please close the door.
Fermez la portière, s'il vous plaît.
Fer-meh la por-tyer, seel voo ple.

I have missed the train!
J'ai manqué le train!
Zheh mahñ-keh luh trañ!

When does the next train leave?
Quand part le prochain train?
Kahñ par luh pro-shañ trañ?

Where is the waiting room?
Où est la salle d'attente?
Oo e la sal da-tahñt?

Where is the lavatory?
Où est le cabinet?
Oo e luh ka-bee-neh?

The train is arriving now.
Le train arrive maintenant.
Luh trañ a-reev mañt-nahñ.

Tickets, please.
Les billets, s'il vous plaît.
Leh bee-yeh, seel voo ple.

All aboard!
En voiture!
Ahñ vwah-tẽur!

The train is leaving.
Le train part.
Luh trañ par.

Arrivals.
Arrivées.
A-ree-veh.

Departures.
Départs.
Deh-par.

Express train.
Le rapide. / L'express.
Luh ra-peed. / Lek-press.

Local train.
Le train omnibus.
Luh trañ om-nee-bẽuss.

Getting Around by Ship and Plane

If you go abroad on a ship or airplane, your first chance to use your French will come in transit. Being able to speak with the personnel can be an exciting start to a journey. They will be more helpful, too, if you make an effort to speak to them in their language. And your efforts will be rewarded.

There's the harbor (the port).
Voilà le port.
Vwah-la luh por.

Where is the pier?
Où est le quai (le débarcadère)?
Oo e luh ke (luh deh-bar-ka-der)?

When does the ship sail?
Quand part le bateau?
Kahñ par luh ba-toh?

Let's go on board!
Montons à bord!
Moñ-toñ a bor!

Where is cabin number . . . ?
Où est la cabine numéro . . . ?
Oo e la ka-been nêû-meh-ro . . . ?

Is this my cabin (stateroom)?
Est-ce ma cabine?
Es ma ka-been?

Steward, do you have the key to my cabin?
Garçon, avez-vous la clé de ma cabine?
Gar-ssoñ, a-veh voo la cleh duh ma ka-been?

I'm looking for the dining room.
Je cherche la salle à manger.
Zhuh shersh la sal a mahñ-zheh.

We want a table for two.
Nous voulons une table pour deux.
Noo voo-loñ zêun tabl poor dôê.

A first-class cabin.
Une cabine de première classe.
Êun ka-been duh pruh-myer klass.

A second-class cabin.
Une cabine de deuxième classe.
Êun ka-been duh dôê-zyem klass.

Let's go on deck.
Allons sur le pont.
A-loñ sêur luh poñ.

I would like a deck chair.
Je voudrais une chaise de pont.
Zhuh voo-dre êun shez duh poñ.

I would like to eat by the swimming pool.
Je voudrais manger près de la piscine.
Zhuh voo-dre mahñ-zheh pre duh la pee-seen.

The ship arrives at seven o'clock.
Le bateau (Le navire) arrive à sept heures.
Luh ba-toh (luh na-veer) a-reev a set ŏer.

When do we go ashore?
Quand est-ce que nous nous débarquons?
Kahñ tes kuh noo noo deh-bar-koñ?

Where is the gangplank?
Où est la passerelle?
Oo e la pass-rel?

The landing card, please.
Le permis de débarquement, s'il vous plaît.
Luh per-mee duh deh-bark-mahñ, seel voo ple.

I wasn't seasick at all!
Je n'avais pas du tout mal de mer!
Zhuh na-ve pah dĕu too mal duh mer!

Have a good trip!
Bon voyage!
Boñ vwah-yahzh!

I want to go to the airport.
Je veux aller à l'aéroport.
Zhuh vŏe za-leh a la-eh-ro-por.

Drive me to the airport.
Conduisez-moi à l'aéroport.
Koñ-deu-ee-zeh mwah a la-eh-ro-por.

When does the plane leave?   **When does it arrive?**
Quand part l'avion?   Quand arrive-t-il?
Kahñ par la-vyoñ?   *Kahñ ta-reev teel?*

Flight number . . . leaves at . . . o'clock.
Le vol numéro . . . part à . . . heures.
Luh vol nĕu-meh-ro . . . par ta . . . ŏer.

From which gate?
De quelle porte?
Duh kel port?

I wish to reconfirm my flight.
Je veux reconfirmer mon vol.
Zhuh vŏè ruh-koñ-feer-meh moñ vol.

Ticket, please.
Le billet, s'il vous plaît.
Luh bee-yeh, seel voo ple.

Boarding pass, please.
Le permis d'embarquer, s'il vous plaît.
Luh per-mee dahñm-bar-keh, seel voo ple.

Please fasten your seat belts.
Attachez les ceintures, s'il vous plaît.
A-ta-sheh leh san-têûr, seel voo ple.

No smoking.
Défense de fumer.
Deh-fahñss duh fêû-meh.

Stewardess, a small pillow, please.
Mademoiselle, un petit oreiller, s'il vous plaît.
Mad-mwah-zel, ŏen puh-tee tor-eh-yeh, seel voo ple.

I fly to Europe every year.
Je vole à l'Europe tous les ans.
Zhuh vol a lŏè-rop too leh zahñ.

The airplane is taking off!
L'avion décolle!
La-vyoñ deh-kol!

Is a meal served during this flight?
Est-ce qu'on sert un repas pendant ce vol?
Es koñ ser ŏen ruh-pah pahñ-dahñ suh vol?

The airplane will land in ten minutes.
L'avion atterrira dans dix minutes.
La-vyoñ a-te-reer-a dahñ dee mee-neût.

There will be a delay.
Il y aura un retard.
Eel ee oh-ra ôeñ ruh-tar.

There's the runway!
Voilà la piste!
Vwah-la la peest!

We have arrived.
Nous sommes arrivés.
Noo som za-ree-veh.

Health

We hope you will never need the phrases you will find in
this section; but emergencies do arise, and sickness does
overwhelm. Since a physician's diagnosis often depends
on what you, the patient, can tell him, you will want to
make your woes clearly understood. If you have a chronic
medical problem, you might well arrange to have various
prescriptions or descriptions of the difficulty in hand or
translated before you leave on your trip.

I need a doctor.
J'ai besoin d'un médecin.
Zheh buh-zwañ dõeñ mehd-sañ.

Send for a doctor.
Faites venir un médecin.
Fet vuh-neer õeñ mehd-sañ.

Are you the doctor?
Êtes-vous le médecin?
Et voo luh mehd-sañ?

What is the matter with you?
Qu'est-ce que vous avez?
Kes kuh voo za-veh?

I don't feel well.
Je ne me sens pas bien.
Zhuh nuh muh sahñ pah byañ.

I'm sick.
Je suis malade.
Zhuh seû-ee ma-lad.

How long have you been sick?
Depuis quand êtes-vous malade?
Duh-peû-ee kahñ et voo ma-lad?

I have a headache.
J'ai mal à la tête.
Zheh mal a la tet.

Where is the hospital?
Où est l'hôpital?
Oo e loh-pee-tal?

Is there a drugstore near here?
Y a-t-il une pharmacie près d'ici?
Ee a teel eûn far-ma-see pre dee-see?

I have a stomach ache.
J'ai mal à l'estomac.
Zheh mal a le-sto-mah.

Do I have a fever?
Est-ce que j'ai une fièvre?
Es kuh zheh eûn fyevr?

I have burned myself.
Je me suis brûlé (*m*) / brûlée (*f*).
Zhuh muh seû-ee breû-leh.

You must stay in bed.
Vous devez garder le lit.
Voo duh-veh gar-deh luh lee.

How long?
Combien de temps?
Kohñm-byañ duh tahñ?

At least two days.
Au moins deux jours.
Oh mwañ dôe zhoor.

Show me your tongue.
Montrez-moi la langue.
Moñ-treh mwah la lahñg.

Lie down.
Couchez-vous.
Koo-sheh voo.

Get up.
Levez-vous.
Luh-veh voo.

Where does it hurt?
Où vous fait-il mal?
Oo voo fe teel mal?

My leg hurts.
La jambe me fait mal.
La zhahñmb muh fe mal.

My finger is bleeding.
Mon doigt saigne.
Moñ dwah seny.

---

the arm, the arms le bras, les bras *luh brah, leh brah*	**the back** le dos *luh doh*
the bladder la vessie *la ve-see*	**the bone** l'os *loss*
the chest la poitrine *la pwah-treen*	**the ear, the ears** l'oreille, les oreilles *lo-rehy, leh zo-rehy*
the elbow le coude *luh kood*	**the eye, the eyes** l'oeil, les yeux *lōē-eey, leh zyōē*
the face le visage *luh vee-zahzh*	**the finger** le doigt *luh dwah*
the foot, the feet le pied, les pieds *luh pyeh, leh pyeh*	**the forehead** le front *luh froñ*

I have a cold.
Je suis enrhumé (m) / enrhumée (f).
Zhuh sêu-ee zahñ-rêu-meh.

Do you smoke?
Fumez-vous?
Fêu-meh voo?

Yes, I smoke.
Oui, je fume.
Wee, zhuh fêum.

No, I don't smoke.
Non, je ne fume pas.
Noñ, zhuh nuh fêum pah.

---

the hair, my hair
les cheveux, mes cheveux
leh shuh-vôe, meh shuh-vôe

the hand, the hands
la main, les mains
la mañ, leh mañ

the head
la tête
la tet

the heart
le coeur
luh kôer

the hip
la hanche
la ahñsh

the joint
l'articulation
lar-tee-kêu-la-syoñ

the kidneys
les reins
leh rañ

the knee
le genou
luh zhuh-noo

the leg, the legs
la jambe, les jambes
la zhahñmb, leh zhahñmb

the liver
le foie
luh fwah

the lung, the lungs
le poumon, les poumons
luh poo-moñ, leh poo-moñ

the mouth
la bouche
la boosh

the muscle
le muscle
luh mêuskl

the neck
le cou
luh koo

Do you sleep well?
Dormez-vous bien?
Dor-meh voo byañ?

No, I don't sleep well.
Non, je ne dors pas bien.
Noñ, zhuh nuh dor pah byañ.

I cough frequently.
Je tousse fréquemment.
Zhuh toos freh-ka-mahñ.

Take this medicine three times a day.
Prenez ce médicament trois fois par jour.
Pruh-neh suh meh-dee-ka-mahñ trwah fwah par zhoor.

the nose le nez *luh neh*	**the shoulder** l'épaule *leh-pohl*
the skin la peau *la poh*	**the skull** le crâne *kuh krahn*
the spine l'épine dorsale *leh-peen dor-sal*	**the stomach** l'estomac *le-sto-mah*
the thigh la cuisse *la kêu-eess*	**the throat** la gorge *la gorzh*
the thumb le pouce *luh pooss*	**the toe** l'orteil *lor-tehy*
the tooth, the teeth la dent, les dents *la dahñ, leh dahñ*	**the waist** la taille *la tah-eey*
the wrist le poignet *luh pwah-nyeh*	

Here is a prescription.
Voici une ordonnance.
Vwah-see ẽun or-do-nahñss.

Can you come again tomorrow?
Pouvez-vous venir encore demain?
Poo-veh voo vuh-neer ahñ-kor duh-mañ?

Yes, I can come.
Oui, je peux venir.
Wee zhuh pŏè vuh-neer.

I will come later.
Je viendrai plus tard.
Zhuh vyañ-dre plẽu tar.

He's a good doctor.
C'est un bon médecin.
Se tŏèñ boñ mehd-sañ.

Sightseeing

No phrase book can possibly supply you with all the phrases you might want in the infinite number of situations, emotions, likes, and dislikes you will encounter in your travels. The basics are here, but they can only be a beginning. The dictionary at the back of this book will supply you with a larger vocabulary to use with the phrases. In addition, local bilingual or multilingual guides are usually very helpful in supplying other language information concerning a given situation. If an unusual phrase is required, ask him and it will be given to you gladly.

I would like to go sightseeing.
Je voudrais aller visiter les curiosités.
Zhuh voo-dre za-leh vee-zee-teh leh kéû-ree-o-zee-teh.

How long does the tour last?
Combien de temps dure le tour?
Koñ-byañ duh tahñ dēur luh toor?

It lasts three hours.
Il dure trois heures.
Eel dēur trwah zōer.

Are you the guide?
Êtes-vous le guide?
Et voo luh geed?

What is the name of this place?
Comment s'appelle cet endroit-ci?
Ko-mahñ sa-pel set ahñ-drwah see?

Are the museums open today?
Est-ce que les musées sont ouverts aujourd'hui?
Es kuh leh mēu-zeh soñ too-ver oh-zhoor-dēu-ee?

No, the museums are closed today.
Non, les musées sont fermés aujourd'hui.
Noñ, leh mēu-zeh soñ jer-meh oh-zhoor-dēu-ee.

The stores are open.
Les magasins sont ouverts.
Leh ma-ga-zañ soñ too-ver.

I would like to visit an art museum.
Je vourdrais visiter un musée d'art.
Zhuh voo-dre vee-zee-teh ōeñ mēu-zeh dar.

Is there an exhibition there now?
Y a-t-il une exposition là maintenant?
Ee a teel ēun eks-po-zee-syoñ la mañt-nahñ?

I would like to see the city.
Je voudrais voir la ville.
Zhuh voo-dre vwar la veel.

What is the name of that church?
Comment s'appelle cette église-là?
Ko-mahñ sa-pel set eh-gleez la?

May we go in?
Pouvons-nous y entrer?
Poo-voñ noo zee ahñ-treh?

Is the old church closed this morning?
La vieille église est-elle fermée ce matin?
La vyehy eh-gleez e tel fer-meh suh ma-tañ?

Will it open this evening?
Sera-t-elle ouverte ce soir?
Suh-ra tel oo-vert suh swar?

This is the main square of the city.
C'est la place principale de la ville.
Se la plass prañ-see-pal duh la veel.

May I take pictures here?
Puis-je prendre des photos ici?
Peu-eezh prahñdr deh fo-to ee-see?

We have walked a lot.
Nous nous sommes promenés beaucoup.
Noo noo som prom-neh boh-koo.

I am tired.
Je suis fatigué (*m*) / fatiguée (*f*).
Zhuh seu-ee fa-tee-geh.

Let's sit down.
Asseyons-nous.
A-seh-yoñ noo.

Where does this street lead to?
Où mène cette rue-ci?
Oo men set reu see?

To the cathedral.
À la cathédrale.
A la ka-teh-dral.

What is that monument?
Quel est ce monument-là?
Kel e suh mo-nêu-mahñ la?

Is that a theater?
Est-ce un théâtre?
Es ᴖeñ teh-ahtr?

It's a movie house.
C'est un cinéma.
Se tᴖeñ see-neh-mah.

What is the name of this park?
Comment s'appelle ce parc-ci?
Ko-mahñ sa-pel suh park see?

We cross the street here.
Nous traversons la rue ici.
Noo tra-ver-ssoñ la rêu ee-see.

Will we visit a castle?
Visiterons-nous un château?
Vee-zee-te-roñ noo ᴖeñ shah-toh?

We will visit a palace.
Nous visiterons un palais.
Noo vee-zee-te-roñ ᴖeñ pa-le.

Who lives in this palace?
Qui habite ce palais?
Kee a-beet suh pa-le?

Nobody lives here.
Personne n'habite ici.
Per-ssoñ na-beet ee-see.

What is the name of this river?
Comment s'appelle ce fleuve?
Ko-mahñ sa-pel suh flᴖeᴗ?

This is the longest bridge in the city.
C'est le pont le plus long de la ville.
Se luh poñ luh plêu loñ duh la veel.

There's too much water in the boat.
Il y a trop d'eau dans le bateau.
Eel ee a tro doh dahñ luh ba-toh.

Is our hotel near the river?
Est-ce que notre hôtel est près du fleuve?
Es kuh notr oh-tel e pre déû flŏev?

This is the shopping center.
C'est le centre d'achats.
Se luh sahñtr dah-shah.

Is it far from here to the beach?
Est-ce loin d'ici à la plage?
Es lwañ dee-see a la plazh?

I would like to go swimming this morning.
Je voudrais aller nager ce matin.
Zhuh voo-dre za-leh na-zheh suh ma-tañ.

If it doesn't rain, we'll go there.
S'il ne pleut pas, nous y irons.
Seel nuh plŏe pah noo zee ee-roñ.

Thank you for an interesting tour.
Je vous remercie d'un tour intéressant.
Zhuh voo ruh-mer-see dŏeñ toor añ-teh-ruh-ssahñ.

Thank you very much for it.
Je vous en remercie beaucoup.
Zhuh voo zahñ ruh-mer-see boh-koo.

I like it.	**I liked it.**
Il me plaît.	Il m'a plu.
Eel muh ple.	*Eel ma plŏû.*

DICTIONARY

Some Tips On French Grammar

Gender Nouns in French are either masculine or feminine. This is important to know, since the form of other parts of speech (definite and indefinite articles, adjectives, pronouns) depends on whether they modify or appear in connection with a masculine or feminine noun. In other words, the definite and indefinite articles (the, a, an) and adjectives always agree with the noun in number and gender. As a general rule, but with a few exceptions, the adjective follows the noun in French. Some adjectives form the feminine irregularly.

Notice the following:

> *un crayon vert*, a green pencil (masculine)
> *des crayons verts*, some green pencils
> *une feuille verte*, a green leaf (feminine)
> *des feuilles vertes*, some green leaves

The definite article (the) is *le* for masculine singular nouns beginning with a consonant, and *l'* for masculine and feminine singular nouns beginning with a vowel, and *la* for feminine singular nouns beginning with a consonant. Before both masculine and feminine plural nouns, the plural definite article *les* is used. The indefinite article (a, an) is *un* for masculine nouns and *une* for feminine nouns.

Notice the following:

> *le crayon vert*, the green pencil (masculine)
> *l'oeil vert*, the green eye (masculine)
> *la feuille verte*, the green leaf (feminine)
> *l'eau verte*, the green water (feminine)
> *les crayons verts*, the green pencils
> *les yeux verts*, the green eyes
> *les feuilles vertes*, the green leaves

Adjectives ending in -*e* have the same form for masculine and feminine.

> *un homme malade*, a sick man (masculine)
> *une femme malade*, a sick woman (feminine)

It is important to remember that when a girl or a women speaks with reference to herself or refers to another female, the feminine form of the adjective must be used.

je suis content, I am glad (man speaking)
je suis contente, I am glad (woman speaking)
il est content, he is glad
elle est contente, she is glad
ils sont contents, they are glad (men or men and women)
elles sont contentes, they are glad (women only)
un couteau jaune, a yellow knife (masculine noun)
une cuillère jaune, a yellow spoon (feminine noun)

Number The plural of nouns and adjectives is normally formed by adding *-s* to the singular. There are some exceptions to this, as indicated below. Note the following:

pomme, apple	*pommes*, apples
dent, tooth	*dents*, teeth
cuillère, spoon	*cuillères*, spoons
cahier, notebook	*cahiers*, notebooks
couteau, knife	*couteaux*, knives
animal, animal	*animaux*, animals

You will note in the pronunciation guides throughout the book that the *-s* or *-x* of the plural is not pronounced.

Verbs Person is indicated in verbs by various endings attached to the verb stem. In certain verb forms, the first and second person singular or the first and third person singular have the same ending. In the regular verbs, the verb stem is got by dropping the *-er*, *-ir*, *-oir*, or *-re* from the infinitive form. A number of verb stems are irregular. The personal pronoun is regularly used in French with the personal endings.

Note the following:

parler, to speak
je parle, I speak
il parle, he speaks
nous parlons, we speak
vous parlez, you speak
ils parlent, they speak

finir, to finish
je finis, I finish
elle finit, she finishes
nous finissons, we finish
vous finissez, you finish
ils finissent, they finish

vendre, to sell
je vends, I sell
il vend, he sells
nous vendons, we sell
vous vendez, you sell
ils vendent, they sell

a, un, une *öen, öun*

able: to be able, pouvoir *poo-vwahr*

aboard, à bord *a bor*

about *adv.,* au sujet de, à propos de *oh séû-zheh duh, a pro-po duh*

about *prep.,* environ *ahñ-vee-rohñ*

above, au-dessus de *oh duh-sséû duh*

abroad, à l'étranger *a leh-trahn-zheh*

absolutely, absolument *ab-so-léû-mahn*

accelerate, accélérer *ak-seh-leh-reh*

accelerator, accélérateur (m) *ak-seh-leh-ra-töer*

accent, *n.,* accent (m) *ak-sahñ*

accept, accepter *ak-sep-teh*

accident, accident (m) *ak-see-dahñ* [13]

according to, selon *suh-lohñ*

account *n.,* compte (m) *kohñt*

ache *n.,* mal (m) *mal* [92]

ache *v.,* faire mal *fer mal*

acquaintance, connaissance (f) *ko-ne-sahñss*

across, à travers *a tra-ver*

act *n.,* acte (m) *akt*

act [do] *v.,* agir *a-zheer;* [perform], jouer *zhooe-eh*

active, actif *ak-teef*

actor, acteur (m) *ak-töer*

actress, actrice (f) *ak-treess*

actual, réel *reh-yel*

add, ajouter *a-zhoo-teh*

address *n.,* adresse (f) *a-dress* [29]

admiration, admiration (f) *ad-mee-ra-syohñ*

admire, admirer *ad-mee-reh*

admission, accès (m) *ak-se*

admit, admettre *ad-metr*

adorable, adorable *a-do-rabl*

advance *v.,* avancer *a-vahñ-seh*

advantage, aventage (m) *a-vahñ-tazh*

adventure, aventure (f) *a-vahñ-téur*

advertisement, publicité (f) *pêu-blee-see-teh*

advice, conseil (m) *kohñ-sehy*

advise, conseiller *kohñ-seh-yeh*

affectionate, affectueux *a-fek-têu-ôe*

afraid: to be afraid, être effrayé, avoir peur *ehtr e-freh-yeh, a-vwahr pôer* [7]

after, après *a-pre*

afternoon, après-midi (m, f) *a-pre-mee-dee*

afterwards, après *a-pre*

again, encore, de nouveau *ahñ-kor, duh noo-voh*

against, contre *kohñtr*

age, âge (m) *ahzh*

agent, agent (m) *a-zhahñ*

ago, il y a *ell ee a*

agree: to be in accord, être d'accord *etr da-kor*

agreeable [pleasing], agréable *a-greh-abl*

agreement, accord (m) *akor*

ahead: straight ahead, tout droit *too drwah*

air, air (m) *er* [74]

air filter, filtre d'air (m) *feeltr der*

air line, ligne aérienne (f) *leeny a-eh-ree-yen*

airmail, par avion *par a-vyohñ*

airplane, avion (m) *a-vyohñ* [88, 89, 90]

airport, aéroport (m) *a-eh-roh-por* [44, 80]

alarm, alarme (f) *a-larm*

alarm clock, réveil (m) *reh-vehy*

alcohol, alcool (m) *al-koh-ol*

alike, semblable *sahñm-blabl*

alive, vivant *vee-vahñ*

all, tout *too* **not at all,** pas du tout *pah dêu too* **after all,** après tout *a-pre too*

allow, permettre *per-metr*

almond, amande (f) *a-mahñd*

almost, presque *presk*

alone, seul *sôel*

along, le long de *luh lohñ duh*

already, déjà *deh-zha* [56]
also, aussi *oh-see*
altar, autel (m) *oh-tel*
alter, changer *shahñ-zheh*
alteration [of clothing], modification (f) *mo-dee-fee-ka-syohñ*
although, bien que *byañ kuh*
altogether, complètement *kong-plet-mahñ*
always, toujours *too-zhoor*
am: I am, je suis *zhuh sēu-ee*
ambassador, ambassadeur (m) *ahm-bas-adōer*
American, Américain *a-meh-ree-kañ*
amount, quantité (f) *kahñ-tee-teh*
amusement, amusement (m) *a-mēuz-mahñ*
amusing, amusant *a-mōe-zahñ*
an, un, une *ōen, ēun*
and, et *eh*
anger *n.,* colère (f) *ko-ler*
angry, en colère, fâché *ahñ ko-ler, fah-sheh*
animal, animal (m) *a-nee-mal*
ankle, cheville (f) *shuh-veey*
announce, announcer *a-nohñ-seh*
annoy, ennuyer *ahñ-nēu-ee-yeh*
another, un autre *ōeñ nohtr*
answer *n.,* réponse (f) *reh-pohñss*
answer *v.,* répondre *reh-pohñdr* [42]
antique shop, chez l'antiquaire *sheh lahñ-tee-ker*
anxious, anxieux *ahñ-zyōe*
any, quelque *kel-kuh*
anyone, quelqu'un *kel-kōen*
anyhow, de toute façon *duh toot fa-ssohñ*
anything, quelque chose, n'importe quoi *kel-kuh shohz, nañ-port kwah*
anywhere, quelque part, n'importe où *kel-kuh par, nan-port oo*
apartment, appartement (m) *a-par-tuh-mahñ*

apologize, s'excuser *sek-skeu-zeh*

apology, excuse (f) *ek-skeuz*

appear, paraître *pa-retr*

appendicitis, appendicite (f) *a-pahñ-dee-seet*

appendix, appendice (m) *a-pahñ-deess*

appetite, appétit (m) *a-peh-tee*

appetizer, apéritif (m) *a-peh-ree-teef*

apple, pomme (f) *pom*

appointment, rendez-vous (m) *rahñ-deh voo*

appreciate, apprécier *a-preh-syeh*

approve, approuver *a-pro-veh*

approximately, approximativement *a-prok-see-ma-teev-mahñ*

April, avril (m) *a-vreel*

arch, arc (m) *ark*

architect, architecte (m) *ar-shee-tekt*

architecture, architecture *ar-shee-tek-teûr*

are: you are, vous êtes *voo zet* **they are,** ils (elles) sont *eel (el) sohñ* **we are,** nous sommes *noo som*

argue, discuter *dees-keû-teh*

arm, bras (m) *brah*

around, autour de *oh-toor duh*

arrange, arranger *a-rahñ-zheh*

arrest *v.*, arrêter *a-re-teh*

arrival, arrivée (f) *a-ree-veh* [85]

arrive, arriver *a-ree-veh* [14, 24, 45, 85, 88, 90]

art, art (m) *ar* [98]

artichoke, artichaut (m) *ar-tee-shoh*

artificial, artificiel *ar-tee-fee-syel*

artist, artiste (m, f) *ar-teest*

as, comme *kom* **as well,** aussi *oh-see*

ashamed, avoir honte *a-vwar ohñt*

ashore, à terre *a ter* **to go ashore,** débarquer *deh-bar-keh* [88]

ashtray, cendrier (m) *sahñ-dree-yeh* [50]

ask, demander *duh-mahñ-deh*

asleep, endormi *ahñ-dor-mee*
asparagus, asperges (m, pl) *ass-perzh*
aspirin, aspirine (f) *ass-pee-reen*
assist, aider *e-deh*
assistant, assistant (m) *a-sees-tahñ*
associate *n.*, associé (m) *a-so-syeh*
association, association (f) *a-so-sya-syohñ*
assure, assurer *a-seû-reh*
at, à *a*
Atlantic, Atlantique (m) *at-lahñ-teek*
attain [reach], atteindre *a-tañdr*
attempt *v.*, essayer *e-seh-yeh*
attend, assister à *a-sees-teh a*
attention, attention (f) *a-tahñ-syohñ*
attract, atirer *a-tee-reh*
audience, spectateurs (m, pl) *spek-ta-tœr*
August, août (m) *oot*
aunt, tante (f) *tahñt*
author, auteur (m) *oh-tœr*
authority, autorité (f) *oh-to-ree-teh*
automobile, automobile (f) *oh-toh-moh-beel*
autumn, automne (m) *oh-ton*
available, disponible *dees-po-neebl*
avenue, avenue (f) *av-neû*
avoid, éviter *eh-vee-teh*
await, attendre *a-tahñdr*
awake *adj.*, éveillé, *eh-veh-yeh*
awake *v.*, éveiller *eh-veh-yeh*
away, au loin, absent *oh lwañ, ab-sahñ*
axle, essieu (m) *e-ssyœ*

baby, bébé (m) *beh-beh*
bachelor, célibataire (m) *seh-lee-ba-ter*
back *adv.*, en arrière *ahñ na-ree-yer* **to go back,** retourner *ruh-toor-neh*
back *n.*, dos (m) *doh*

bacon, lard (m) *lar*

bad, mauvais *moh-ve*

badly, mal *mal*

bag, sac (m) *sak*

baggage, bagages (m) *bag-gahzh* [83]

baggage check, bulletin de bagages (m) *beûl-tañ duh bah-gahzh* [83]

bakery, boulangerie (f) *boo-lahñ-zhuh-ree*

balcony, balcon (m) *bal-kohñ*

ball, balle (f) *bal*

banana, banane (f) *ba-nan*

band [music], orchestre (m) *or-kestr*

bandage, bandage (m) *bahñ-dahzh*

bank, banque (f) *bahñk* [29]

bar, bar (m) *bar*

barber, barbier (m), coiffeur (m) *bar-byeh, kwah-föer*

bargain *n.*, occasion (f) *oh-ka-zyohñ*

basket, panier (m) *pa-nyeh*

bath, bain (m) *bañ* [36]

bathe, se baigner *suh ben-yeh*

bathing suit, costume de bain (m) *kos-teûm duh bañ*

bathroom, salle de bain (f) *sal duh bañ* [38]

battery, batterie (f) *ba-tree*

bay, baie (f) *be*

be, être *etr*

beach, plage (f) *plahzh* [101]

bean, haricot (m) *a-ree-koh*

beard, barbe (f) *barb*

beautiful, beau (m), belle (f) *boh, bel* [9]

beauty parlor, salon de beauté (m) *sa-lohñ duh boh-teh*

because, parce que *parss kuh*

become, devenir *duh-vuh-neer*

bed, lit (m) *lee* [92] **to go to bed,** se coucher, aller au lit *suh koo-sheh, a-leh oh lee*

bedroom, chambre à coucher (f) *shahñmbr a koo-sheh*

bee, abeille (f) *a-behy*

beef, boeuf (m) *bœf*

beefsteak, bifteck *beef-tehk*

beer, bière (f) *byer* [55]

beet, betterave (f) *bet-rahv*

before [time], avant *a-vahñ;* [place], devant *duh-vahñ*

begin, commencer *ko-mahñ-seh*

beginning, commencement (m) *koh-mahns-mahñ*

behind, derrière *de-ree-yer*

believe, croire *krwar*

bell, cloche (f) *klosh*

belong, appartenir *a-par-tuh-neer*

belt, ceinture (f) *sañ-tēūr* [73, 89]

beside, à côté de *a koh-teh duh*

besides, d'ailleurs *dah-yōèr*

best, le meilleur *luh meh-yōèr*

better *adj.,* meilleur *meh-yōèr*

better *adv.,* mieux *myōè*

between, entre *ahñtr*

big, grand *grahñ* [68]

bill, addition (f), note (f) *a-dee-syohñ, not* [56, 69]

bird, oiseau (m) *wah-zoh*

birth, naissance (f) *ne-ssahnss*

birthday, anniversaire (m) *a-nee-ver-ser*

bit: a bit, un peu *ōèñ pōè*

bite *v.,* mordre *mordr*

black, noir *nwar* [68]

blanket, couverture (f) *koo-ver-tēūr*

bleed, saigner *se-nyeh* [93]

blind, aveugle *ah-vōègl*

blister, ampoule (f) *ahñ-pool*

block *n.,* bloc (m) *blok*

blonde, blond (m), blonde (f) *blohñ, blohñd*

blood, sang (m) *sahñ*

blouse, blouse (f) *blooz*

blue, bleu *blōè*

board: room and board, pension (f) *pahñ-syohñ*

boarding house, pension (f) *pahñ-syohñ*

boarding pass, permis d'embarquement (m) *per-mee dahñ-bark-mahñ* [89]

boat, bateau (m) *ba-toh* [101]

body, corps (m) *kor*

boil *v.,* bouillir *boo-ee-yeer*

bone, os (m) *oss*

book, livre (m) *leevr*

bookstore, librairie (f) *lee-bre-ree*

booth, cabine (f) *ka-been*

boot, botte (f) *bot*

border *n.,* frontière (f) *frohñ-tyer*

born: to be born, né, être né *neh, etr neh*

borrow, emprunter *ahñ-prŏeñ-teh*

both, les deux *leh dŏè*

bottle, bouteille (f) *boo-tehy* [55]

bottle opener, ouvre-bouteille (m) *oovr boo-tehy*

bottom, fond (m) *fohñ*

box, boîte (f) *bwaht* [00]

boy, garçon (m) *gar-ssohñ*

bracelet, bracelet (m) *bra-ssuh-leh*

brake, frein (m) *frañ*

brandy, cognac (m) *kon-yak*

brassiere, soutien-gorge (m) *soo-tyañ-gorzh*

brave, brave *brahv*

bread, pain (m) *pañ*

break *v.,* casser, rompre, briser *ka-seh, rohñmpr, bree-zeh*

breakfast, petit déjeuner (m) *puh-tee deh-zhŏè-eh* [37, 48]

breast, poitrine (f) *pwah-treen*

breath, respiration (f) *re-spee-rah-syohñ*

breathe, respirer *res-pee-reh*

bridge, pont (m) *pohñ* [100]

bright, clair, *kler*

bring, apporter *a-por-teh* [11, 50, 51, 53, 54]

broken, cassé, rompu, brisé *ka-seh, rohñm-pŏû, bree-zeh*

brother, frère (m) *frer* [2]

brown, brun *brŏeñ*
bruise n., contusion (f) *kohñ-teû-zyohñ*
brush n., brosse (f) *bross*
brunette, brunet *brêu-neh*
build v., construire *kohñ-strêu-eer*
building, édifice (m) *eh-dee-feess*
burn n., brûlure (f) *brêu-lêur*
burn v., brûler *brêu-leh* [92]
burst v., éclater *eh-klah-teh*
bus, autobus *oh-toh-bêuss* [14, 45, 46]
business, affaire (f) *a-fer*
busy, occupé *o-kêu-peh* [42]
but, mais *me*
butter, beurre (m) *bŏer* [50, 51, 53]
button, bouton (m) *boo-tohñ*
buy, acheter *ash-teh* [65, 69]
by, par *par*

cabbage, chou (m) *shoo*
cabin, cabine (f) *ka-been* [87]
café, café (m) *ka-feh*
cake, gâteau (m) *gah-toh*
call n., visite (f) *vee-zeet*
call v., appeler *ap-leh* [14, 38, 43]
camera, appareil photographique (m) *a-pa-rehy fo-to-gra-feek*
can n., boîte de conserve (f) *bwaht duh kohñ-serv*
can: to be able, pouvoir *poo-vwar* **I can,** je peux *zhuh pŏe*
canal, canal (m) *ka-nal*
cancel v., annuler *a-nêu-leh*
candy, bonbon (m) *bohñ-bohñ*
candy store, boutique de confiseur (f) *boo-teek duh kohñ-fee-zŏer*
capital, capital (f) *ka-pee-tal*
car, voiture (f) *vwah-têur* [72, 74, 76]

carburetor, carburateur *kar-bêû-ra-tôer*
card, carte (f) *kart* [37]
care *n.*, soin (m) *swañ*
care *v.*, se soucier *suh soo-syeh*
careful, soigneux *swah-nyôè*
carpet, tapis (m) *ta-pee*
carrot, carotte (f) *ka-rot*
carry, porter *por-teh* [34]
cash *n.*, argent comptant *ar-zhahñ kohñ-tahñ*
cash *v.*, changer *shahñ-zheh* [30]
cashier, caissier *ke-syeh* [56]
castle, château (m) *shah-toh* [100]
cat, chat (m) *shah*
catch *v.*, attraper *a-tra-peh*
cathedral, cathédrale (f) *ka-teh-dral* [100]
Catholic, catholique *ka-to-leek*
catsup, sauce tomate (f) *sohss to-mat*
cattle, bétail (m) *beh-tah-eey*
cauliflower, choufleur (m) *shoo-flôer*
caution, précaution (f) *preh-koh-syohñ*
cave, caverne (f) *ka-vern*
ceiling, plafond (m) *pla-fohñ*
celery, céleri (m) *seh-luh-ree*
cellar, cave (f) *kav*
cemetery, cimetière (m) *seem-tyer*
center, centre (m) *sahñtr*
centimeter, centimètre (m) *sahñ-tee-metr*
century, siècle (m) *syekl*
ceremony, cérémonie (f) *seh-reh-moh-nee*
certain, certain *ser-tañ*
certainly, certainement *ser-ten-mahñ*
chair, chaise (f) *shez*
chambermaid, femme de chambre (f) *fam duh shahñmbr* [38]
champagne, champagne (m) *shahñm-pany*
chance *n.*, chance (f) *shahñss*

change [coins], monnaie (f) *mo-neh* [31]

change *v.*, changer *shahñ-zheh* [30, 31]

chapel, chapelle (f) *sha-pel*

charge *v.*, compter *kohñ-teh*

charming, charmant *shar-mahñ*

chauffeur, chauffeur (m) *shoh-föer*

cheap, bon marché *bohñ mar-sheh* [66]

check *n.*, chèque (m) *shek* [30,56] **traveler's check,**
chèque de voyageurs *shek duh vwah-ya-shöer* [30]

check [one's luggage], faire enregistrer *fer ahñ-re-zhees-
treh* [83]

check [inspect], vérifier *veh-ree-fyeh*

cheek, joue (f) *zhoo*

cheese, fromage (m) *fro-mahzh*

cherry, cerise (f) *suh-reez*

chest, poitrine (f) *pwah-treen*

chicken, poulet (m) *poo-leh*

child, enfant (m) *ahñ-fahñ*

chin, menton (m) *mahñ-tohñ*

chocolate, chocolat (m) *sho-ko-lah*

choose, choisir *shwah-zeer*

chop, côtelette (f) *koht-let*

Christmas, Noël (m) *noh-el*

church, église (f) *eh-gleez* [99]

cigar, cigare (m) *see-gar*

cigarette, cigarette (f) *see-gar-et* [33, 69]

cinema, cinéma *see-neh-ma*

circle, cercle (m) *serkl*

citizen, citoyen, citoyenne *see-twah-yañ*, *see-twah-yen*

city, ville (f) *veel* [98, 99, 100]

class, classe (f) *klass* **first class,** première classe *pruh-
myer klass* **second class,** deuxième classe *döè-zyem
klass*

classify, classifier *kla-see-fyeh*

clean *adj.*, propre *propr* [39, 54, 55]

clean *v.*, nettoyer *ne-twah-yeh*

cleaners, teinturier (m) *tañ-téû-ree-yeh*

clear, clair *kler*

climb, grimper *grañm-peh*

clock, pendule (f) *pahñ-déûl*

close [near], près *pre*

close *v.,* fermer *fer-meh* [33, 38, 61, 84]

closed, fermé *fer-meh* [98, 99]

closet, placard (m), armoire (f) *pla-kar, ar-mwar*

cloth, drap (m), toile (f) *drah, twahl*

clothes, vêtements (m) *vet-mahñ*

cloud, nuage (m) *néû-ahzh* [7]

clutch [of a car], embrayage (m) *ahñ-breh-yahzh*

coast, côte (f) *koht*

coat [topcoat], pardessus (m) *par-duh-sséû*; [suitcoat], veston (m) *ves-tohñ*

cocktail, cocktail (m) *kok-tel*

coffee, café (m) *ka-feh* [50, 51, 52]

cognac, cognac (m) *koñ-yak*

coin, pièce de monnaie (f) *pyess duh mo-neh* [42]

cold *adj.,* froid *frwah* [51, 52]   **I am cold,** j'ai froid *zhe frwah*   **it is cold,** il fait froid *eel fe frwah*

cold *n.,* rhume (m) *réûm* [94]

collar, col (m) *kol*

collect, rassembler *ra-sahñm-bleh*

collection, collection (f) *ko-lek-syohñ*

college, collège (m) *ko-lezh*

collide, se heurter *suh óer-teh*

color, couleur (f) *koo-lóer* [67]

comb, peigne (m) *peny*

come, venir *vuh-neer* [12, 96]   **come here!** venez ici! *vuh-neh ee-see*   **come in!** entrez! *ahñ-treh*

comfortable, confortable *kohñ-for-tabl*

company, compagnie (f) *kohñm-pa-nyee*

comparison, comparaison (f) *kohñ-pa-re-zohñ*

compartment, compartiment (m) *kohñ-par-tee-mahñ*

complain, se plaindre *suh plañdr*

complete *adj.*, complet *kohñm-pleh*
compliment *n.*, compliment *kohñm-plee-mahñ*
concert, concert (m) *kohñ-ser*
condition, condition (f) *kohñ-dee-syohñ*
confuse, rendre confus, déconcerter *rahñdr kohñfeû, deh-kohñ-ser-teh*
congratulations, félicitations *feh-lee-see-ta-syohñ*
connect, lier, rattacher *lee-yeh, ra-ta-sheh*
consent *v.*, consentir *kohñ-sahñ-teer*
consider, considérer *kohñ-see-deh-reh*
constipated, constipé *kohñ-stee-peh*
consul, consul (m) *kohñ-seûl*
consulate, consulat (m) *kohñ-seû-lah*
contagious, contagieux *kohñ-ta-zhœ̀*
contain, contenir *kohñ-tuh-neer*
contented, content *kohñ-tahñ*
continue, continuer *kohñ-tee-neû-eh*
contrary, contraire *kohñ-trer* **on the contrary,** au contraire *oh kohñ-trer*
convenient, pratique *pra-teek*
conversation, conversation (f) *kohñ-ver-sa-syohñ*
cook *n.*, cuisinière (f) *kēû-ee-zee-nyer*
cook *v.*, faire la cuisine, cuire, faire cuire *fer la kēû-ee-zeen, kēû-eer, fer kēû-eer*
cool, frais, fraîche *fre, fresh* [6]
copy, copie (f) *ko-pee*
corkscrew, tire-bouchon (m) *teer-boo-shohñ*
corn, mais (m) *mah-eess*
corner, coin (m) *kwañ*
correct *adj.*, correct *ko-rekt*
cost *n.*, prix (m) *pree*
cost *v.*, coûter *koo-teh* [66, 72]
cotton, coton (m) *ko-tohñ*
cough *n.*, toux (f) *too*
cough *v.*, tousser *too-seh* [95]
count *v.*, compter *kohñ-teh* [31]

country, pays (m), campagne (f) *peh-ee, kahñ-pany* [73]

courage, courage (m) *koo-rahzh*

course, cours (m) *koor* **of course**, bien entendu *byañ nahñ-tahn-dẽu* **main course**, plat de résistance (m) *plah duh reh-zees-tahñss*

court, tribunal (m) *tree-bẽu-nal*

courtyard, cour (f) *koor* [36]

cover v., couvrir *koo-vreer*

cow, vache (f) *vash*

crab, crabe (m) *krab*

cramp, crampe (f) *krahñmp*

crazy, fou, folle *foo, fol*

cream, crème *krem*

cross n., croix (f) *krwah*

cross v., traverser *tra-ver-seh* [100]

crossing, croisement *krwahz-mahñ;* [by ship], traversée (f) *tra-ver-seh*

crossroads, croisement de chemins *krwahz-mahñ duh shu-mañ*

crowd, foule (f) *fool*

cry v., pleurer *plõe-reh*

cucumber, concombre (m) *kohñ-kohñmbr*

cup, tasse (f) *tass* [52]

curve, tournant (m), courbe (f) *toor-nahñ, koorb*

custard, flan (m) *flahñ*

customer, client *klee-ahñ*

customs, douane (f) *doo-ahn*

cut [wound], coupure (f) *koo-peẽur*

cut v., couper *koo-peh*

cutlet, côtelette (f) *koht-let*

daily, *adv.*, journellement, quotidien *zhoor-nel-mahñ, koh-tee-dyañ*

damage v., endommager *ahñ-do-ma-zheh*

damp, humide *ẽu-meed* [6]

dance *n.*, danse (f) *dahñss*
dance *v.*, danser *dahñ-seh*
danger, danger (m) *dahñ-zheh*
dangerous, dangereux *dahñ-zhuh-rôê*
dare *v.*, oser *oh-zeh*
dark, obscur, foncé *ob-skéùr, fohñ-seh*
darkness, obscurité (f) *ohb-skéù-ree-teh*
date [time], date (f) *dat;* [appointment], rendez-vous (m)
    rahñ-deh-voo
daughter, fille (f) *feey* [2]
day, jour (m) *zhoor* **per day, a day,** par jour *par zhoor*
dead, mort, *mor*
dear [endearment], cher, chère *sher*
December, décembre (m) *deh-sahñmbr*
decide, décider *deh-see-deh*
deck, pont (m) *pohñ* [87]
declare, déclarer *deh-kla-reh* [32]
deep, profond *proh-fohñ*
deer, cerf (m) *serf*
delay *n.*, délai (m), retard (m) *deh-le, ruh-tar* [90]
delicious, délicieux *deh-lee-syôê*
delighted, enchanté *ahñ-shahñ-teh*
deliver, délivrer *deh-lee-vreh*
dentist, dentiste (m) *dahñ-teest*
deodorant, déodorisant (m) *deh-oh-doh-ree-zahñ*
department store, grand magasin (m) *grahñ ma-ga-zañ*
departure, départ (m) *deh-par* [85]
deposit *v.*, déposer *deh-po-zeh* [42]
descend, descendre *de-sahñdr*
describe, décrire *deh-kreer*
desert *n.*, désert (m) *deh-zer*
desert *v.*, déserter *deh-zer-teh*
desire *v.*, désirer *deh-zee-reh*
desk, bureau (m) *béù-roh*
dessert, dessert (m) *de-sser* [55]

destroy, détruire *deh-treû-eer*

detour, détour (m), déviation (f) *deh-toor, deh-vee-ya-syohñ*

develop, développer *deh-vlo-peh*

dial *v.,* composer un numéro *kohñm-po-zeh 6eñ neû-meh-roh* [41, 42]

diamond, diamant (m) *dee-a-mahñ*

diaper, lange (m) *lahñzh*

diarrhea, diarrhée (f) *dee-a-reh*

dictionary, dictionnaire (m) *deek-syoh-ner*

die *v.,* mourir *moo-reer*

difference, différence (f) *dee-feh-rahñss*

different, différent *dee-feh-rahñ*

difficult, difficle *dee-fee-seel*

dine, dîner *dee-neh* [53]

dining car, wagon-restaurant (m) *va-gohñ re-stoh-rahñ* [54]

diningroom, salle à manger (f) *sal a mahñ-zheh* [37, 87]

dinner, dîner (m) *dee-neh* [48, 50]

direct, direct *dee-rekt*

direction, direction (f) *dee-rek-syohñ*

director, directeur (m) *dee-rek-tôer*

dirty, sale *sal* [52]

disappear, disparaître *dees-pa-retr*

discount *n.,* remise (f) *ruh-meez* [70]

discuss, discuter *dees-keû-teh*

disease, maladie (f) *ma-la-dee*

dish, plat (m), assiette (f) *plah, ass-yet*

disinfect, désinfecter *deh-zañ-fek-teh*

distance, distance (f) *dees-tahñss*

district, district (m) *dees-treekt*

disturb, déranger *deh-rahñ-zheh*

divorced, divorcé *dee-vor-seh*

do, faire *fer* **how do you do?** Comment vous portez-vous? *ko-mahñ voo por-teh voo?*

dock, quai (m) *ke*

doctor, docteur (m), médecin (m) *dok-tôer, mehd-sañ* [14, 92, 96]

dog, chien (m) *shyañ*

doll, poupée (f) *poo-peh*

dollar, dollar (m) *do-lar* [30]

done, fait *fe*

door, porte (f) *port* [84]

dose, dose (f) *doz*

double, double *doobl*

doubt, doute (m) *doot* **without doubt,** sans doute *sahñ doot*

down, en bas *ahñ bah* **to go down,** descendre *de-sahñdr*

downtown, centre de la ville (m) *sahñtr duh la veel* [45]

dozen, douzaine (f) *doo-zen*

drawer, tiroir (m) *teer-war*

dress *n.,* robe (f) *rob* [68]

dress [oneself], s'habiller *sa-bee-yeh*

dressmaker, couturier (m), couturière (f) *koo-têur-yeh, koo-têur-yer*

drink *n.,* boisson (f) *bwah-sohñ*

drink *v.,* boire *bwar*

drive *v.,* conduire *kohñ-dêu-eer* [44, 76]

driver, chauffeur (m) *shoh-fôer* [43]

drop *v.,* laisser tomber *le-seh tohñm-beh*

druggist, pharmacien (m) *far-ma-syañ*

drugstore, pharmacie (f) *far-ma-see* [92]

drunk, ivre, soûl *eevr, soo*

dry, sec, sèche *sek, sesh*

duck, canard (m) *ka-nar*

during, pendant *pahñ-dahñ*

dust, poussière (f) *poo-syer*

duty, devoir (m) *duh-vwar;* [tax], droits de douane (m, pl) *drwah duh doo-ahn* [33]

dysentery, dysenterie (f) *dee-zahñ-tuh-ree*

each, chaque *shak*
each one, chacun *shak-ŏèn*
eager, ardent *ar-dahñ*
ear, oreille (f) *or-ehy*
earache, mal à l'oreille *mal a lor-ehy*
early, tôt, de bonne heure *toh, duh bon ŏèr* [23]
earn, gagner *ga-nyeh*
earring, boucle d'oreille *bookl dor-ehy*
earth, terre (f) *ter*
easily, facilement *fa-seel-mahñ*
east, est (m) *est*
Easter, Pâques (f, pl) *pahk*
easy, facile *fa-seel*
eat, manger *mahñ-zheh* [37, 48, 55]
edge, bord (m) *bor*
egg, oeuf (m) *ŏèf*
eight, huit *ŭ-eet*
eighteen, dix-huit *deez-ŭ-eet*
eighth, huitième *ŭ-ee-tyem*
eighty, quatre-vingts *katr vañ*
either . . . or, ou . . . ou *oo . . . oo*
elbow, coude (m) *kood*
electric, électrique *eh-lek-treek*
elevator, ascenseur (m) *a-sañh-sŏèr* [38]
eleven, onze *ohñz*
else: nobody else, personne d'autre *per-son dohtr* **nothing else,** rien d'autre *ree-añ dohtr* **something else,** quelque chose d'autre *kel-kuh shohz dohtr*
elsewhere, ailleurs *ah-ee-yŏèr*
embark, s'embarquer *sahñm-bar-keh*
embarrassed, embarassé *ahñm-ba-ra-seh*
embassy, ambassade (f) *ahñm-ba-sad*
embrace *v.,* embrasser *ahñm-bra-seh*
emergency, urgence (f) *ŭr-zhahñss*
empty, vide *veed*

end *n.*, fin (f) *fañ*
engaged [busy], occupé *o-keû-peh*
engine, moteur (m) *moh-tôèr*
English, anglais *ahn-gle* [10]
enjoy, s'amuser *sa-meû-zeh*
enormous, énorme *eh-norm*
enough, assez *a-seh* **that's enough**, cela suffit *suh-la seû-fee*
enter, entrer *ahñ-treh*
entertaining, amusant *a-meû-zahñ*
entire, entier *ahñ-tyeh*
entrance, entrée (f) *ahñ-treh*
envelope, enveloppe (f) *ahñ-vlop*
equal, égal *eh-gal*
equipment, équipement (m) *eh-keep-mahñ*
error, erreur (f) *e-rôèr*
Europe, Europe *ôe-rop*
even *adv.*, même *mem*
even [number], pair *per*
evening, soirée (f) *swa-reh* [99] **good evening**, bon soir *bohñ swar*
ever, jamais *zha-me*
every, chaque *shahk*
everyone, chacun, tout le monde *sha-kôeñ, too luh mohñd*
everything, tout *too*
everywhere, partout *par-too*
evidently, évidemment *eh-vee-da-mahñ*
exact, exact *eg-zakt*
examination, examen (m) *eg-za-mañ*
examine, examiner *eg-za-mee-neh*
example, example (m) *eg-zahñm-pl* **for example**, par example *par eg-zahñmpl*
excellent, excellent *ek-se-lahñ*
except, excepté *ek-sep-teh*
exchange *v.*, échanger *eh-shahñ-zheh*
exchange rate, cours (m) *koor* [30]

excursion, excursion (f) *ek-skeur-zyohñ*

excuse *v.,* excuser *ek-skeu-zeh* **excuse me,** pardon *pardohñ*

exercise, exercice (m) *eg-zer-seess*

exhibition, exposition (f) *ek-spoh-zee-syohñ* [98]

exit, sortie (f) *sor-tee*

expect, espérer *es-peh-reh*

expensive, cher, chère *sher* [37, 66]

explain, expliquer *ek-splee-keh*

explanation, explication (f) *ek-splee-ka-syohñ*

export *v.,* exporter *eks-por-teh*

express *adj.,* express *ek-spress* [85]

extra, extra *ek-strah*

extraordinary, extraordinaire *ek-stra-or-dee-ner*

eye, oeil (m) *ôê-eey*

face, visage (m) *vee-zahzh*

factory, usine (f) *êû-zeen*

faint *v.,* s'évanouir *seh-va-noo-eer*

fair [market], foire (f) *fwar*

fall [season], automne (m) *oh-ton*

fall *n.,* chute (f) *shêut*

fall *v.,* tomber *tohñm-beh*

false, faux, fausse *foh, fohss*

family, famille (f) *fa-meey*

famous, fameux *fa-môê*

fan, éventail (m) *eh-vahñ-tah-eey*

far, loin *lwañ* **so far,** jusqu'à présent *zhêùs-ka preh-zahñ* **how far is it?** à quelle distance? *a kel dees-tahñss*

fare [cost], tarif (m) *ta-reef*

farewell, adieu (m) *a-dyôê*

farm, ferme (f) *ferm*

farmer, fermier (m) *fer-myeh*

farther, plus loin *plêu lwañ*

fashion, mode (f) *mod*

fast [quick], vite *veet*

fasten, fixer *feek-seh*
fat, gras, grasse *grah, grahss*
father, père (m) *per* [2]
father-in-law, beau-père (m) *boh-per*
fault, faute (f) *foht*
favor, faveur (f) *fa-võer*
favorite *adj., & n.,* favori (m) *fa-vo-ree*
fear: to be afraid, avoir peur *a-vwar põer*
feather, plume (f) *pleûm*
February, février (m) *feh-vree-yeh*
fee, honoraires (m, pl) *o-no-rer*
feel, sentir *sahñ-teer* [92]
feeling, sentiment (m) *sahñ-tee-mahñ*
female, femelle *fe-mel*
fence, barrière (f) *ba-ree-yer*
fender, garde-boue (m) *gard-boo*
ferry [boat], bac (m) *bak*
fever, fièvre (f) *fyevr* [92]
few, quelques *kel-kuh*
field, champ (m) *shahñ*
fifteen, quinze *kañz*
fifth, cinquième *sañ-kyem*
fifty, cinquante *sañ-kahñt*
fight *n.,* combat (m) *kohñm-bah*
fight *v.,* se battre *suh ba-tr*
fill *v.,* remplir *rahñm-pleer* [37]
filling [for a tooth], plombage (m) *plohñm-bahzh*
film, film (m) *feelm*
final, final *fee-nal*
finally, finalement, enfin *fee-nal-mahñ, ahñ-fañ*
find, trouver *troo-veh*
fine *adj.,* parfait *par-fe*
fine *n.,* amende (f) *a-mahñd* [75]
finger, doigt (m) *dwah* [93]
finish *v.,* finir *fee-neer*
fire, feu (m) *fõe* [14]

first, premier *pruh-myeh* **first class,** première classes *pruh-myer klass* [83]

fish *n.,* poisson (m) *pwah-ssohñ* [55]

fish *v.,* pêcher *pe-sheh*

fish-bone, arête (f) *a-ret*

fit [seizure], accès (m) *ak-se*

fit *v.,* convenir *kohñ-vuh-neer*

fitting [of a garment], essayage (m) *e-seh-yahzh*

five, cinq *sañk*

fix *v.,* aranger, reparer *a-rahñ-zheh, reh-pa-reh* [74, 76]

flag, drapeau (m) *dra-poh*

flashbulb, ampoule photographique (f) *ahñm-pool foh-toh-gra-feek*

flat, plat *plah*

flat tire, pneu crevé (m) *pnõe kruh-veh* [74]

flavor, bouquet (m), saveur (f) *boo-keh, sa-võer*

flight, vol (m) *vol* [88, 89]

flint, silex (m) *see-leks*

flirt *v.,* flirter *fleer-teh*

flood, inondation (f) *ee-nohñ-dah-syohñ*

floor, plancher (m), étage (m) *plahñ-sheh, eh-tahzh*

florist, fleuriste (m) *flõer-eest*

flower, fleur (f) *flõer*

fluid, fluide (m) *flêu-eed*

fly [insect], mouche (f) *moosh*

fly *v.,* voler *vo-leh* [89]

fog, brouillard (m) *broo-ee-yar* [5]

follow, suivre *sêu-eevr*

food, nourriture (f), aliments (m, pl) *noo-ree-teur, a-lee-mahñ*

foot, pied (m) *pyeh*

for, pour *poor*

forbid, défendre *deh-fahñdr*

forbidden, défendu, interdit *deh-fahñ-dêu, añ-ter-dee*

forehead, front (m) *frohñ*

foreign, étranger *eh-trahñ-zheh*

foreigner, étranger *eh-trahñ-zheh*
forest, forêt (f) *fo-reh*
forget, oublier *oo-blee-yeh*
forgive, pardonner *par-do-neh*
fork, fourchette (f) *foor-shet* [54]
form, forme (f) *form*
former, antérieur *ahñ-teh-ree-ōer*
formerly, précédemment, jadis *preh-seh-da-mahñ, zha-dee*
fort, fort (m) *for*
fortunate, heureux *ōe-rōe*
fortunately, heureusement *ōe-rōez-mahñ*
forty, quarante *ka-rahñt*
forward, en avant *ahñ na-vahñ*
fountain, fontaine (f) *fohñ-ten*
four, quatre *katr*
fourteen, quatorze *ka-torz*
fourth, quatrième *ka-tree-yem*
fracture *n.,* fracture (f) *frak-tēur*
fragile, fragile *frah-zheel*
free, libre *leebr* [43]
freedom, liberté (f) *lee-ber-teh*
freeze, geler *zhuh-leh*
French, français *frahñ-se*
frequently, fréquemment *freh-ka-mahñ*
fresh, frais, fraîche *fre, fresh* [51]
Friday, vendredi (m) *vahñ-druh-dee*
fried, frit *free*
friend, ami *a-mee* [2]
friendly, amical *a-mee-kal*
from, de *duh*
front, devant (m) *duh-vahñ*   **in front of,** devant *duh-vahñ*
frozen, glacé, gelé *gla-seh, zhuh-leh*
fruit, fruit (m) *frēu-ee* [51]
full, plein *plañ*
fun, amusement (m) *a-mēuz-mahñ*
function, fonction (f) *fohñk-syohñ*

funnel, entonnoir (m) *ahñ-ton-nwar*
funny, drôle *drohl*
fur, fourrure (f) *foo-rêur*
furnished, meublé *mōēb-leh*
furniture, meubles (m, pl) *mōēbl*
further, ultérieur *êul-teh-ree-yōēr*
future, futur (m), *avenir* (m) *fêu-têur, a-vuh-neer*

gain *v.,* gagner *ga-nyeh*
gamble *v.,* jouer *zhoo-eh*
game, jeu (m) *zhōē*
gangplank, passerelle (f) *pass-rel* [88]
garage, garage (m) *ga-rahzh* [76]
garden, jardin (m) *zhar-dañ*
garlic, ail (m) *ah-eey*
gas, gaz (m) *gaz*
gasoline, essence (f) *e-sahñss* [73, 74]
gas station, station de service (f), poste d'essence (m)
    sta-syohñ duh ser-veess, post de-sahñss [73]
gate, barrière (f) *ba-ree-yer* [89]
gather [collect], ramasser *rah-mah-seh*
gay, gai *ge*
general *adj.,* général (m) *zheh-neh-ral* **in general,**
    généralement *zheh-neh-ral-mahñ*
generous, généreux *zheh-neh-rōē*
gentleman, monsieur *muh-syōē*
get, obtenir *ob-tuh-neer* **get in,** entrer *ahñ-tre* **get
    off,** descendre *de-sahñdr* [45] **get on,** monter *mohñ-
    teh* [45] **get up,** se lever *suh luh-veh* [24, 93]
gift, cadeau (m) *ka-doh*
gin, gin (m) *zheen*
girl, jeune fille (f) *zhōēn feey* [9]
give, donner *do-neh* [11] **give me,** donnez-moi *do-neh
    mwah*
glad, content *kohñ-tahñ*

gladly, avec plaisir, volontiers *a-vek pleh-zeer, voh-lohñ-tyeh*

glass [for drinking], verre (m) *ver* [51, 54, 55]

glasses [for the eyes], lunettes (f, pl) *leū-net*

glove, gant (m) *gahñ*

go, aller *a-leh* [11, 34, 43, 45, 87, 101] **go back,** revenir *ruh-vuh-neer* **go in,** entrer *ahñ-treh* **go out,** sortir *sor-teer*

God, Dieu (m) *dyōe*

gold, or (m) *or*

good, bon *bohñ*

good bye, au revoir *oh ruh-vwar*

government, gouvernement (m) *goo-ver-nuh-mahñ*

grandfather, grand-père *grahñ-per*

grandmother, grand'mère *grahñ-mer*

grapes, raisins (m) *re-zañ*

grapefruit, pamplemousse (m) *pahñmpl-mooss*

grass, herbe (f) *erb*

grateful, reconnaissant *ruh-ko-ne-sahñ*

gray, gris *gree*

grease *n.*, graisse (f) *gress*

great, grand *grahñ*

green, vert *ver*

grocery, épicerie (f) *eh-pees-ree*

ground, sol (m) *sol*

group, groupe (m) *groop*

grow, cultiver *keūl-tee-veh*

guard *n.*, gardien (m) *gar-dyañ*

guest, invité *añ-vee-teh*

guide *n.*, guide (m) *geed* [98]

guilty, coupable *koo-pahbl*

guitar, guitare (f) *gee-tar*

gum, gomme (f) *gom*

gun, fusil (m) *feū-zey*

habit, habitude (f) *ah-bee-teūd*

hair, cheveux (m, pl) *shuh-vōe*

haircut, coupe de cheveux (f) *koop duh shuh-vóē*
hairdresser, coiffeur (m) *kwah-fóēr*
hairpin, épingle à cheveux (f) *eh-pañgl a shuh-vóē*
half *adj.*, demi *duh-mee*
half *n.*, moitié (f) *mwah-tyeh*
hall, salle (f) *sal*
ham, jambon (m) *zhahñm-bohñ*
hand, main (f) *mañ*
handkerchief, mouchoir (m) *moo-shwar* [39]
hand-made, fait à la main *fe ta la mañ*
handsome, beau, bel, belle *boh, bel, bel* [9]
hang, accrocher *akro-sheh* **hang up**, pendre *pahñdr*
hanger [for clothing], porte-manteau (m) *port-mahñ-toh*
happen, arriver, se passer *a-ree-veh, suh pass-eh* [14]
happy, heureux *óē-róē*
harbor, port (m) *por* [86]
hard [with difficulty], difficile *dee-fee-seel;* [quality], dur *déūr*
hardly [not likely], à peine *a pen*
harm *n.*, dommage (m), mal (m) *do-mahzh, mal*
harm *v.*, faire du mal à, nuir à *fer déū mal a, néū-eer a*
harmful, nuisible *néū-ee-zeebl*
haste, hâte (f) *aht*
hat, chapeau (m) *sha-poh*
hat shop, chapelier *sha-puh-lee-yeh*
hate *v.*, haïr *ah-eer*
have, avoir *a-vwar* **I have**, j'ai *zheh* **have you?** avez-vous? *a-veh voo?*
he, il *eel*
head, tête (f) *tet*
headache, mal à la tête *mal a la tet* [92]
health, santé (f) *sahñ-teh* [55]
hear, entendre *ahñ-tahñdr*
heart, coeur (m) *kóēr*
heat *n.*, chaleur (f) *sha-lóēr*
heavy, lourd *loor*

heel, talon (m) *ta-lohñ*
hello, bonjour, allô *bohñ-zhoor, a-loh*
help *n.*, secours (m), aide (f) *suh-koor, ed*
help *v.*, aider *e-deh* [13]
helpful, utile *êû-teel*
hem *n.*, ourlet (m) *oor-leh*
hen, poule (f) *pool*
her *adj.*, son, sa *sohñ, sa*
here, ici *ee-see*
hers, le sien, la sienne *luh syañ, la syen*
high, haut *oh*
hill, colline (f) *ko-leen*
him, le *luh* **to him,** lui *lêû-ee*
hip, hanche (f) *ahñsh*
hire, louer *loo-eh* [72]
his, son, sa *sohñ, sa*
history, histoire (f) *ees-twar*
hit *v.*, frapper *fra-peh*
hold, tenir *tuh-neer*
hole, trou (m) *troo*
holiday, vacances (f, pl), fête (f) *va-kahñss, fet*
holy, saint *sañ*
home, maison (f), domicile (m) *me-zohñ, do-mee-seel*
honest, honnête *o-net*
honey [food], miel (m) *myel*
honor, honneur (m) *o-nêèr*
hope *n.*, espoir (m) *e-spwar*
hope *v.*, espérer *e-speh-reh* [3]
horn [automobile], klaxon (m) *klak-sohñ*
hors d'oeuvres, hors d'oeuvres *or-dêèvr*
horse, cheval (m) *shuh-val*
hospital, hôpital (m) *oh-pee-tal* [92]
host, hôte *oht*
hot, chaud *shoh*
hotel, hôtel (m) *oh-tel* [9, 31, 35, 37, 44, 53, 69, 101]
hour, heure (f) *êèr*

house, maison (f) *me-zohñ*

how, comment *ko-mahñ* **how are you?** comment allez-vous? *ko-mahñ ta-leh-voo* **how far?** à quelle distance? *a kel dees-tahñss* **how long?** combien de temps? *kohñm-byañ duh tahñ* **how many?** combien? *kohñm-byañ* **how much?** combien? *kohñ-byañ*

hug *n.,* étreinte (f) *eh-trañt*

human, humain *êu-mañ*

humid, humide *êu-meed*

hundred, cent *sahñ*

hunger, faim (f) *fañ*

hungry: to be hungry, avoir faim *a-vwar fañ* [47, 48]

hurry *v.,* se dépêcher *suh deh-pe-sheh* [13] **to be in a hurry,** être pressé *etr pre-seh*

hurt, faire mal *fer mal* [93]

husband, mari (m) *ma-ree* [2]

I, je, moi *zhuh, mwah*

ice, glace (f) *glass* [55]

ice cream, glace (f) *glass* [55]

idea, idée (f) *ee-deh*

identification, identification (f) *ee-dahñ-tee-fee-ka-syohñ*

if, si *see*

ill, malade *ma-lad*

illegal, illégal *eel-leh-gal*

illness, maladie (f) *ma-la-dee*

imagine, imaginer *ee-ma-zhee-neh*

immediately, immédiatement, tout de suite *ee-meh-dyat-mahñ, too duh sêu-eet*

important, important *añm-por-tahñ*

impossible, impossible *añm-po-seebl* [12]

improve, améliorer *a-meh-lee-yo-reh*

improvement, amélioration (f) *a-meh-lee-yo-ra-syohñ*

in, dans, en *dahñ, ahñ*

incident, incident (m) *añ-see-dahñ*

included, inclus, compris *añ-klêu, kohñm-pree* [56]

incomplete, incomplet *añ-koñm-ple*
inconvenient, incommode *añ-ko-mod*
incorrect, incorrect *añ-ko-rekt*
increase *v.,* augmentation (f) *ohg-mahñ-tah-syohñ*
incredible, incroyable *añ-krwah-yabl*
indeed, en effet *ahñ neh-feh*
independence, indépendance (f) *añ-deh-pahñ-dahñss*
independent, indépendant *añ-deh-pahñ-dahñ*
indicate, indiquer *añ-dee-keh*
indigestion, indigestion (f) *añ-dee-zhes-tyohñ*
indoors, à l'intérieur *a lañ-teh-ree-ŏèr*
industrial, industriel *añ-dŏès-tree-yel*
inexpensive, bon marché *bohñ mar-sheh*
infection, infection (f) *añ-fek-syohñ*
infectious, infectieux *añ-fek-tee-ŏè*
inform, informer *añ-for-meh*
information, renseignements (m, pl) *rahñ-seny-mahñ*
injection, injection (f) *añ-zhek-syohñ*
injury, blessure (f) *ble-sĕur*
injustice, injustice (f) *añ-zhĕus-teess*
ink, encre (f) *ahñkr*
inn, auberge (f) *oh-berzh*
inquire, demander *duh-mahñ-deh*
inside, intérieur, dedans *añ-teh-ree-ŏèr, duh-dahñ*
insist, insister *añ-sees-teh*
inspect, inspecter *añ-spek-teh* [74]
instead of, au lieu de *oh-lyŏè duh*
institution, institution (f) *añ-stee-tĕu-syohñ*
insurance, assurance (f) *a-sĕu-rahñss* [73]
insure, assurer *a-sĕu-reh*
intelligent, intelligent *an-te-lee-zhahñ*
intend, avoir l'intention de *a-vwar lañ-tahñ-syohñ duh*
intense, intense *añ-tahñss*
intention, intention (f) *añ-tahñ-syohñ*
interest *n.,* intérêt (m) *añ-teh-re*
interest *v.,* intéresser *añ-teh-re-seh*

interesting, intéressant, e *añ-teh-re-sahñ* [101]
intermission, entr'acte (m) *ahñtr-akt*
internal, interne *añ-tern*
international, international *añ-ter-nah-syo-nal*
interpret, interpréter *añ-ter-preh-teh*
interpreter, interprète (m) *añ-ter-pret*
interview *n.*, entrevue (f) *añtr-véu*
into, dans *dahñ*
introduce, présenter *preh-zahñ-teh*
introduction, introduction (f) *añ-tro-déuk-syohñ*
investigate, rechercher *ruh-sher-sheh*
invitation, invitation (f) *añ-vee-tah-syohñ*
invite, inviter *añ-vee-teh*
iron [for ironing], fer à repasser (m) *fer a ruh-pass-eh*
iron [metal], fer (m) *fer*
iron *v.*, repasser *ruh-pass-eh*
is, est *e* **he is**, il est *eel e* **she is**, elle est *el e* **it is**, il est, elle est, c'est *eel e, el e, se*
island, île (f) *eel*
itch *v.*, démanger *deh-mahñ-zheh*

jacket, jaquette (f) *zha-ket* [6]
jail, prison (f) *pree-zohñ*
jam, confiture (f) *kohñ-fee-téur*
January, janvier *zhahñ-vyeh*
jaw, mâchoire (f) *mah-shwar*
jelly, gelée (f) *zhuh-leh*
jewelry, bijouterie (f) *bee-zhoo-tree*
jewelry store, bijouterie (f) *bee-zhoo-tree*
job, travail (m) *tra-vah-eey*
joke, plaisanterie (f) *ple-zahñ-tree*
juice, jus (m) *zhéu*
July, juillet (m) *zhéu-ee-yeh*
jump *v.*, sauter *soh-teh*
June, juin *zhéu-añ*

just, juste *zhêust*
justice, justice (f) *zhêus-teess*

keep, garder *gar-deh*
key, clé (f) *kleh* [33, 38, 73, 87]
kidneys, reins(m) *rañ*
kill, tuer *têu-eh*
kilogram, kilo *kee-loh*
kilometer, kilomètre (m) *kee-loh-metr* [72]
kind *adj.,* aimable *e-mabl*
kind *n.,* espèce (f) *es-pess* [30]
king, roi (m) *rwah*
kiss *n.,* baiser (m) *be-zeh*
kitchen, cuisine (f) *kêu-ee-zeen*
knee, genou (m) *zhuh-noo*
knife, couteau (m) *koo-toh* [53]
knock *v.,* frapper *fra-peh*
know [something], savoir *sa-vwar* [9]; [someone], connaître *ko-netr* [9]

laborer, ouvrier *oo-vree-yeh*
lace, dentelle (f) *dahñ-tel*
ladies' room, Dames *dahm*
lady, dame (f) *dahm*
lake, lac (m) *lak*
lamb, agneau (m) *a-nyoh*
lame, boiteux *bwah-tôè*
lamp, lampe (f) *lahñmp*
land *n.,* terre (f) *ter*
land *v.,* atterrir *a-te-reer* [90]
landing card, carte de débarquement (f) *kart duh deh-bark-mahñ* [88]
language, langue (f) *lahñg*
large, grand *grahñ*
last *adj.,* dernier *der-nyeh*

last *v.*, durer *déû-reh* [98]
late, tard *tar* [23, 84]
laugh *v.*, rire *reer*
laughter, risée (f) *ree-zeh*
laundry, blanchisserie (f) *blahñ-shee-suh-ree*
lavatory, cabinet (m) *ka-bee-neh* [85]
law, loi (f) *lwah*
lawyer, avocat (m) *a-voh-kah*
lazy, paresseux *pa-ruh-sóê*
lead *v.*, mener *muh-neh* [99]
leaf, feuille (f) *fóê-eey*
leak *n.*, fuite (f) *féû-eet*
learn, apprendre *a-prahñdr*
least, moindre *mwañdr*
leather, cuir (m) *kéû-eer*
leave, laisser, partir *les-eh, par-teer* [14, 24, 39, 46, 83, 85, 86, 88]
left, gauche (f) *gohsh* [44]
leg, jambe (f) *zhahñmb* [93]
lemon, citron (m) *see-trohñ*
lend, prêter *pre-teh*
length, longueur *lohñ-góêr*
lens, lentille (f) *lahñ-teey*
less, moins *mwañ*
let, permettre *per-metr*
letter, lettre (f) *letr* [39]
lettuce, laitue (f) *le-téû*
liberty, liberté (f) *lee-ber-teh*
library, bibliothèque (f) *bee-blee-oh-tek*
license, licence (f), permis (m) *lee-sahñss, per-mee* [76]
lie [untruth], mensonge (m) *mahñ-sohñzh*
lie: to lie down, se coucher *suh koo-sheh* [93]
lie *v.*, mentir *mahñ-teer*
life, vie (f) *vee*
lift *v.*, lever *luh-veh*
light [weight], léger *leh-zheh*

light, lumière (f) *lêu-myer*

lighter [cigarette], briquet (m) *bree-keh*

lightning, éclairs (m, pl), foudre (f) *eh-kler, foodr* [7]

like *adj.*, comme *kom*

like *v.*, aimer *e-meh* [35] **I would like,** je voudrais *zhuh voo-dre*

line, ligne (f) *leeny* [42]

linen, linge (m) *lañzh*

lip, lèvre (f) *levr*

lipstick, rouge à lèvres (m) *roozh ah levr*

liqueur, liqueur (f) *lee-kȫer*

list, liste (f) *leest*

listen, écouter *eh-koo-teh*

liter, litre *leetr* [74]

little, petit *puh-tee* **a little,** un peu *ȫñ pȫe*

live *v.*, vivre, demeurer, habiter *veevr, duh-mȏè-reh, a-bee-teh* [9, 100]

liver, foie (m) *fwah*

lobby, entrée (f), foyer (m) *ahñ-treh, fwah-yeh*

lobster, homard (m) *oh-mahr*

long, long *lohñ* [68]

look *v.*, regarder *ruh-gar-deh*

loose, détaché *deh-ta-sheh* [68]

lose, perdre *perdr* [14, 38]

lost, perdu *per-dȇu*

lot: a lot of, beaucoup de *boh-koo duh* [99]

lotion, friction (f) *freek-syohñ*

loud, bruyant *brȇu-ee-yahñ*

love *n.*, amour (m) *a-moor*

love *v.*, aimer *e-meh* [9]

low, bas *bah*

lubricate *v.*, lubrifier *lêu-bree-fee-yeh*

luck, chance (f) *shahñss* **good luck,** bonne chance *bon shahñss*

lucky, fortuné *for-tȇu-neh* **to be lucky,** avoir de la chance *a-vwar duh la shahñss*

luggage, bagages (m, pl) *bah-gahzh* [34, 39, 43, 83]

lunch, déjeuner (m) *deh-zhoê-neh* [48]

lung, poumon (m) *poo-mohñ*

machine, machine (f) *ma-sheen*

madam, madame *ma-dahm*

magazine, revue (f) *ruh-veû*

mail *n.*, courrier (m) *koo-ree-yeh*

mailbox, boîte aux lettres (f) *bwaht oh letr*

main, principal *prañ-see-pal* **main course,** plat de résistance (m) *plah duh reh-zees-tahñss*

major, majeur *ma-zhoêr*

make, faire *fer*

male, mâle (m) *mahl*

man, homme *om* [9, 14]

manager, directeur (m) *dee-rek-toêr*

manicure, manucure (f) *ma-neû-keûr*

manner, manière (f) *ma-nyer*

manufactured, manufacturé *ma-neû-fak-teû-reh*

many, beaucoup *boh-koo*

map, carte géographique (f), carte routière (f) *kart zheh-oh-gra-feek, kart roo-tyer* [75]

marble, marbre (m) *marbr*

March, mars (m) *marss*

mark, marque (f) *mark*

market, marché (m) *mar-sheh*

marketplace, place du marché (f) *plass deû mar-sheh*

marmalade, confiture (f) *kohñ-fee-teûr*

married, marié *ma-ree-yeh*

marry, épouser *eh-poo-zeh*

marvelous, merveilleux *mer-veh-yoê*

mass [church], messe (f) *mess*

massage *n.*, massage (m) *mah-sahzh*

match, allumette (f) *a-leû-met* [69]

material, tissu (m) *tee-seû*

matter: no matter, n'importe *nañm-port* **what is the matter?** de quoi s'agit-il? qu'y a-t-il? *duh kwah sah-zhee-teel? kee a teel?*

May, mai (m) *me*

may, pouvoir *poo-vwar* **I may,** je peux *zhuh pŏè* **may I?** puis-je? *pê̂u-eezh*

maybe, peut-etre *pŏèt-etr*

me, me, moi *muh, mwah* **to me,** me, moi *muh, mwah*

meal, repas (m) *ruh-pah* [37, 48, 53]

mean *v.,* signifier, vouloir dire *see-nyee-fee-yeh, vool-war deer* [12]

measure *n.,* mesure (f) *muh-zéûr*

measure *v.,* mesurer *meh-zéû-reh*

meat, viande (f) *vyahñd* [55]

mechanic, mécanicien (m) *meh-ka-nee-syañ* [74]

medicine, médecine (f), médicament (m) *mehd-zeen, meh-dee-ka-mahñ* [95]

medium, moyen (m) *mwah-yañ*

meet, rencontrer *rahñ-kohñ-treh* [3, 24]

melon, melon (m) *muh-lohñ*

member, membre (m) *mahñmbr*

memory, mémoire (f) *meh-mwar*

mend, raccommoder *ra-ko-mo-deh*

men's room, Messieurs *meh-syŏè*

mention *v.,* mentionner *mahñ-syo-neh*

menu, menu (m), carte (f) *muh-nêu, kart*

message, message (m) *me-sahzh*

messenger, messager (m) *me-sah-zheh*

metal, métal (m) *meh-tal*

meter [measure], mètre (m) *metr*

middle, milieu (m) *mee-lyŏè*

midnight, minuit (m) *mee-nêu-ee* [23]

mild, doux *doo*

milk, lait (m) *le* [51, 52]

milliner, modiste (f) *mo-deest*

million, million (m) *mee-lyohñ*

mind, esprit (m) *e-spree*

mine, le mien, la mienne *luh myañ, la myen*

mineral, minéral *mee-neh-ral*

mineral water, eau minérale (f) *oh mee-neh-ral*

minute, minute (f) *mee-neût*

mirror, miroir (m) *meer-war* [73]

misfortune, malheur (m) *mal-ŏer*

Miss, Mademoiselle *mad-mwah-zel*

missing, perdu, égaré *per-dêù, eh-ga-reh*

mistake *n.,* faute (f), erreur (f) *foht, e-rŏer* [56]

mistaken, trompé *trohñm-peh*

mix *v.,* mélanger *meh-lahñ-zheh*

mixed, mélangé *meh-lahñ-zheh*

model, modèle (m) *mo-del*

modern, moderne *mo-dern*

modest, modeste *mo-dest*

moment, moment (m) *mo-mahñ*

Monday, lundi (m) *lŏeñ-dee*

money, argent (m) *ar-zhahñ* [14, 30, 31]

money order, mandat postal (m) *mahñ-dah pos-tal*

monk, moine (m) *mwahn*

month, mois (m) *mwah* **per month, a month,** par mois *par mwah*

monument, monument (m) *mo-nêù-mahñ* [100]

moon, lune (f) *lêun* [7]

more, plus *plêù*

morning, matin (m) *ma-tañ* [101] **good morning,** bonjour *bohñ-zhoor*

mosquito, moustique (m) *moos-teek*

mosquito net, moustiquaire *moos-tee-ker*

most, le plus *luh plêù* **most of,** la plupart *la plêù-par*

mother, mère (f) *mer* [2]

motion, mouvement (m) *moov-mahñ*

motor, moteur (m) *moh-tŏer*

mountain, montagne (f) *mohñ-tany*

mouth, bouche (f) *boosh*

move *v.,* bouger *boo-zheh* [15]

movie, cinéma (m) *see-neh-mah* [100]

Mr., Monsieur *muh-syôe*

Mrs., Madame *ma-dahm*

much, beaucoup *boh-koo* **too much,** trop *troh* **how much?** combien? *kohñm-byañ*

mud, boue (f) *boo*

muffler, pot d'échappement (m) *poh deh-shahp-mahñ*

muscle, muscle (m) *mêûskl*

museum, musée (m) *mêû-zeh* [45, 98]

mushroom, champignon (m) *shahñm-pee-nyohñ*

music, musique (f) *mêû-zeek*

musician, musicien *mêû-zee-syañ*

must, devoir *duh-vwar* **I must,** je dois, il me faut *zhuh dwah, eel muh foh*

mustache, moustache (f) *moos-tahsh*

mustard, moutarde (f) *moo-tard*

mutton, mouton (m) *moo-tohñ*

my, mon, ma, mes *mohñ, ma, meh*

myself, moi-même *mwah-mem*

nail [fingernail], ongle (m) *ohñgl*

nail file, lime à ongles (f) *leem a ohñgl*

naked, nu *nêû*

name, nom (m) *nohñ* **last name,** nom de famille (m) *nohñ duh fa-meey* **what is your name?** Comment vous appelez-vous? *ko-mahñ voo zap-leh voo?* **my name is . . . ,** je m'appelle . . . *zhuh ma-pel . . .*

napkin, serviette (f) *ser-vee-yet* [54]

narrow, étroit *eh-trwah* [68]

nation, nation (f) *nah-syohñ*

national, national *nah-syoh-nal*

nationality, nationalité (f) *nah-syo-na-lee-teh*

native, indigène *añ-dee-zhen*

natural, naturel *na-têû-rel*

naturally, naturellement *na-téû-rel-mahñ*
nature, nature (f) *na-téûr*
near, près *pre*
nearly, presque *presk*
necessary, nécessaire *neh-se-ser*
neck, cou (m) *koo*
necklace, collier (m) *ko-lyeh*
necktie, cravate (f) *krah-vaht*
need *v.*, avoir besoin de *a-vwar buh-zwañ duh* [11]   **I need,**
   j'ai besoin de . . . *zheh buh-zwan duh*
needle, aiguille (f) *e-géû-eey* [69]
neighbor, voisin *vwah-zañ*
neighborhood, voisinage (m) *vwah-zee-nahzh*
neither . . . nor . . . , ni . . . ni . . . *nee . . . nee*
nephew, neveu (m) *nuh-vóè*
nerve, nerf (m) *nerf*
nervous, nerveux *ner-vóè*
never, jamais *zha-me*
nevertheless, néanmoins *neh-ahñ-mwañ*
new, nouveau *noo-voh*
news, nouvelles (f, pl) *noo-vel*
newspaper, journal (m) *zhoor-nal*
next *adj.*, prochain *pro-shañ* [85]
next *adv.*, ensuite *ahñ-séû-eet*
nice, gentil *zhahñ-teey*
niece, nièce (f) *nyes*
night, nuit (f) *néû-ee* **good night,** bonne nuit *bon néû-ee*
nightclub, boîte de nuit (f) *bwaht duh néû-see*
nightgown, chemise de nuit (f) *shuh-meez duh néû-ee*
nine, neuf *nóèf*
nineteen, dix-neuf *deez-nóèf*
ninety, quatre-vingt-dix *katr-vañ-deess*
ninth, neuvième *nóè-vyem*
no, non *nohñ*
noise, bruit (m) *bréû-ee*
noisy, bruyant *bréû-ee-yahñ*

none [of persons], personne *per-son;* [of things], rien *ree-yañ*

noodles, nouilles (f, pl) *noo-eey*

noon, midi (m) *mee-dee* [23]

no one, personne, ne . . . personne, personne ne *per-son, nuh . . per-son, per-son nuh*

north, nord (m) *nor*

northeast, nord-est (m) *nord-est*

northwest, nord-ouest (m) *nord-oo-est*

nose, nez (m) *neh*

not, ne . . . pas *nuh . . . pah*

notebook, cahier (m) *kah-yeh*

nothing, rien *ree-yañ* **nothing else,** rien de plus *ree-yañ duh plêûs*

notice *n.,* avis (m) *a-vee*

notice *v.,* remarquer *ruh-mar-keh*

notify, notifier *no-tee-fee-yeh*

novel [book], roman (m) *ro-mahñ*

November, novembre (m) *no-vahñmbr*

novocaine, novocaine (f) *no-vo-ka-een*

now, maintenant *mañt-nahñ*

nowhere, nulle part *nêul par*

number, numéro (m) *nêùmeh-roh* [38, 41]

nun, nonne (f) *non*

nurse, infirmière (f) *añ-feer-myer*

nursemaid, nourrice (f) *noo-reess*

nut, noix (f) *nwah*

obey, obéir *oh-beh-eer*

obliged, obligé *ob-lee-zheh*

obtain, obtenir *ob-tuh-neer*

obvious, évident *eh-vee-dahñ*

occasionally, de temps en temps *duh tahñ zahñ tahñ*

occupation, occupation (f) *o-kêù-pah-syohñ*

occupied, occupé *o-kêù-peh* [84]

ocean, océan (m) *o-seh-ahñ* [36]

October, octobre (m) *ok-tobr*

odd [unusual], étrange *eh-trahñzh*

odd [number], impair *añ-per*

of, de *duh*

offer *v.*, offrir *of-reer*

office, bureau (m) *bêu-roh*

official *adj.*, officiel *o-fee-syel*

often, souvent *soo-vahñ*

oil, huile (f) *êu-eel* [74]

old, vieux *vyôe*

olive, olive (f) *o-leev*

omelet, omelette (f) *om-let*

on, sur *sêur*

once, une fois *êun, fwah*

one, un, une *ôen êun*

one way [street], sens unique *sahñss êu-neek*; [ticket], billet aller (m) *bee-yeh a-leh*

onion, oignon (m) *o-nyohñ*

only, seulement, ne . . . que *sêul-mahñ, nuh . . . kuh*

open *adj.*, ouvert *oo-ver* [98]

open *v.*, ouvrir *oov-reer* [33, 38, 61, 84, 88, 89]

opera, opéra (m) *o-peh-rah*

operation, opération (f) *o-peh-rah-syohñ*

operator [telephone], téléphoniste (f) *teh-leh-fon-eest*

opinion, opinion (f) *o-pee-nyohñ*

opportunity, occasion (f) *o-kah-zyohñ*

opposite, en face de *ahñ fass duh*

optician, opticien (m) *op-tee-syañ*

or, ou *oo*

orange, orange (f) *oh-rahñzh*

order *v.*, commander *ko-mahñ-deh* [55]

ordinary, ordinaire *or-dee-ner*

oriental, oriental *o-ree-yahñ-tal*

original, original *o-ree-zhee-nal*

ornament, ornement (m) *or-nuh-mahñ*

other, autre *ohtr*

ought, devoir *duh-vwar*

our, notre *notr*

ours, le nôtre *luh nohtr*

out *adv.,* hors *or* **to go out,** sortir *sor-teer*

outdoor, dehors *duh-or*

out of order, dérangé *deh-rahñ-zheh*

outside *adv.,* hors de *or* duh **outside of,** en dehors de *ahñ duh-or duh*

over [ended] *adj.,* terminé *ter-mee-neh*

over [above] *prep.,* au-dessus *oh-duh-sêu*

overcharge *n.,* faire payer trop cher *fer peh-yeh troh sher*

overcoat [man's], pardessus (m); [woman's], manteau (m) *par-duh-sêu, mahñ-toh*

overcooked, trop cuit *troh kêu-ee*

overhead, au-dessus *oh-duh-sêu*

overturn, renverser *rahñ-ver-seh*

owe, devoir *duh-vwar* [56]

own *adj.,* propre *prohpr*

owner, propriétaire (m) *proh-pree-yeh-ter*

oyster, huître (f) *êu-eetr*

pack *v.,* empaqueter, emballer *ahñ-pa-kuh-teh, ahñ-ba-leh* [69]

package, paquet (m) *pa-keh*

page, page (f) *pahzh*

paid, payé *peh-yeh*

pain, douleur (f) *doo-lôer*

paint, peinture (f) *pañ-têur*

paint *v.,* peindre *pañdr*

painting, peinture (f) *peñ-têur*

pair, paire (f) *per* [68]

palace, palais (m) *pa-le* [100]

pale, pâle *pahl*

palm, palmier (m) *pahl-myeh*

pants, pantalon (m) *pahñ-ta-lohñ*

paper, papier (m) *pa-pyeh*

parcel, paquet (m) *pa-keh*

pardon, pardon (m) *par-dohñ* **pardon me,** pardonnez-moi *par-do-neh mwah*

parents, parents (m) *pa-rahñ*

park *n.,* parc (m) *park* [100]

park [a car] *v.,* stationner *sta-syo-neh* [76]

parsley, persil (m) *per-seel*

part, pièce (f) *pyess*

part [leave] *v.,* partir *par-teer*

particular, particulier *par-tee-kêû-lee-yeh*

partner [business], associé *a-so-syeh*

party, partie (f), soirée (f) *par-tee, swa-reh*

pass *v.,* passer *pass-eh*

passage, passage (m) *pah-sahzh*

passenger, passager *pah-sah-zheh*

passport, passeport (m) *pass-por* [14, 15, 30, 32, 33]

past, passé (m) *pass-eh*

pastry, pâtrisserie (f) *pah-tees-ree*

path, sentier *sahñ-tyeh*

patient *adj.,* patient *pa-syahñ*

patient *n.,* malade (m, f) *ma-lad*

pay *v.,* payer *peh-yeh* [33, 56, 75] **to pay cash,** payer comptant *peh-yeh kohñ-tahñ* [70]

payment, paiement (m) *peh-mahñ*

peace, paix (f) *pe*

peaceful, tranquille *trahñ-keel*

peach, pêche (f) *pesh*

peak, pic (m) *peek*

peanut, cacahuète *ka-ka-êûet*

pear, poire (f) *pwar*

pearl, perle (f) *perl*

peasant, paysan *peh-ee-zahñ*

peas, pois (m), petits pois *pwah, puh-tee pwah*

peculiar, étrange *eh-trahñzh*

pen, plume (f) *plêûm* **fountain pen,** stylo (m) *stee-loh*

penalty, punition (f) *péû-nee-syohñ*
penny, centime (m) *sahñ-teem*
people, gens *zhahñ*
pepper [spice], poivre (m) *pwahvr*
peppermint, menthe (f) *mahñt*
per, par *par*
perfect, parfait *par-fe*
performance [theatre], représentation (f) *ruh-preh-zahñ-tah-syohñ*
perfume, parfum (m) *par-fôeñ*
perfumery, parfumerie (f) *par-feû-muh-ree*
perhaps, peut-être *pôèt-etr*
period, période (f) *peh-ree-yod*
permanent, permanet *per-ma-nahñ*
permission, permission (f) *per-mee-syohñ*
permit *v.,* permettre *per-metr*
person, personne (f) *per-son*
personal, personnel *per-so-nel* [33]
perspiration, transpiration (f) *trahñ-spee-rah-syohñ*
petrol, essence (f) *e-sahñss*
petticoat, jupon (m) *zhéû-pohñ*
pharmacist, pharmacien (m) *fahr-mah-syañ*
pharmacy, pharmacie (f) *fahr-mah-see*
photograph, photo (f) *foh-toh*
photographer, photographe (m) *foh-toh-graf*
photography, photographie (f) *foh-toh-gra-fee*
photography shop, magasin de photographie (m) *ma-ga-zañ duh foh-toh-gra-fee*
piano, piano (m) *pee-ya-noh*
pick [choose], choisir *shwah-zeer*
pick up *v.,* cueillir *kéû-eh-yeer*
picture, image (f), tableau (m) *ee-mahzh, tab-loh*
pie [pastry], tarte (f) *tart;* [meat], pâté (m) *pah-teh*
piece, morceau (m) *mor-soh*
pier, jetée (f), quai (m) *zhuh-teh, ke* [86]
pig, porc, cochon (m) *por, ko-shohñ*

pigeon, pigeon (m) *pee-zhohñ*

pile, tas (m) *tah*

pill, pilule (f) *pee-lêul*

pillar, pilier (m) colonne (f) *pee-lyeh, ko-lon*

pillow, oreiller (m) *o-reh-yeh* [89]

pilot, pilote (m) *pee-lot*

pin, épingle (f) *eh-pañgl* [69] **safety pin,** épingle de sûreté (f) *eh-pañgl duh sêur-teh*

pineapple, ananas (m) *a-na-na*

pink, rose *roz*

pipe [tobacco], pipe (f) *peep*

place n., place (f), endroit (m) *plass, ahñ-drwah* [98]

place v., mettre, poser *metr, poh-zeh*

plain [simple], *sañmpl*

plan n., plan (m) *plahñ*

plant, plante (f) *plahñt*

plastic, plastique (m) *plas-teek*

plate, assiette (f) *a-syet*

platform, plateforme (f), quai (m) *plat-form, ke* [83]

play v., jouer *zhoo-eh*

pleasant, agréable *a-greh-yabl*

please [suit or satisfy], plaire à *pler a* **if you please,** s'il vous plaît *seel voo ple*

pleasure, plaisir (m) *pleh-zeer* [3]

plenty of, beaucoup de *boh-koo duh*

plum, prune (f) *prêun*

pneumonia, pneumonie (f) *pnôe-mo-nee*

poached, poché *po-sheh*

pocket, poche (f) *posh*

pocketbook [purse], sac à main, portefeuille (f) *sak a mañ, port-fôe-eey*

point n., point *pwañ*

poison, poison (m) *pwah-zohñ*

poisonous, vénéneux *veh-neh-nôe*

police, police (f) *po-leess* [14]

police man, agent de police *a-zhahñ duh po-leess*

police station, commissariat de police *ko-mee-sa-ree-ah duh po-leess*

political, politique *po-lee-teek*

pond, étang (m) *eh-tahñ*

pool, piscine (f) *pee-seen*

poor, pauvre *pohvr*

popular, populaire *po-pêu-ler*

pork, porc (m) *por*

port, port (m) *por* [86]

porter, facteur (m) *fak-tôêr* [34, 82, 83]

portrait, portrait (m) *por-tre*

position, situation (f) *see-têu-ah-syohñ*

positive, certain *ser-tañ*

possible, possible *po-seebl* [12]

possibly, probablement *pro-ba-bluh-mahñ*

postage, affranchissement (m) *a-frahñ-sheess-mahñ*

postage stamp, timbre-poste (m) *tañmbr-post* [39]

postcard, carte postale (f) *kart pos-tal*

post office, poste (f), bureau de poste (m) *post, bêu-roh duh post*

potato, pomme de terre (f) *pom duh ter*

pound [money], livre (f) *leevr*

powder, poudre (f) *poodr*

power, puissance (f) *pêu-ee-sahñss*

powerful, puissant *pêu-ee-sahñ*

practical, pratique *pra-teek*

practice n., entraînement (m) *ahñ-tren-mahñ*

prayer, prière (f) *pree-yer*

precious, précieux *preh-syôê*

prefer, préférer *preh-feh-reh*

preferable, préférable *preh-feh-rabl*

pregnant, enceinte *ahñ-sañt*

premier, premier ministre *pruh-myeh mee-neestr*

preparation, préparation (f) *preh-pah-rah-syohñ*

prepare, préparer *preh-pa-reh*

prepay, payer à l'avance *peh-yeh a la-vahñss*

prescription, ordonnance (f) *or-do-nahñss* [96]
present [gift], cadeau (m) *ka-doh;* [time], présent (m) *preh-zahñ*
present *v.,* présenter *preh-zahñ-teh* [2]
press [clothes] *v.,* repasser *ruh-pass-eh*
pressure, pression (f) *pre-syohñ*
pretty, joli *zho-lee* [9]
prevent, empêcher *ahñ-pe-sheh*
previous, précédent *preh-seh-dahñ*
price, prix (m) *pree*
priest, prêtre (m) *pretr*
principal, principal *prañ-see-pal*
prison, prison (f) *pree-zohñ*
prisoner, prisonnier *pree-zo-nyeh*
private, privé *pree-veh*
prize, prix (m) *pree*
probable, probable *proh-babl*
probably, probablement *proh-bah-bluh-mahñ*
problem, problème (m) *proh-blem*
produce *v.,* produire *proh-dêu-eer*
production, production (f) *proh-dêuk-syohñ*
profession, profession (f) *proh-fe-syohñ*
professor, professeur (m, f) *proh-fe-sóer*
profit, profit (m) *proh-fee*
program *n.,* programme (m) *proh-grahm*
progress *n.,* progrès (m) *proh-gre*
promenade, promenade (f) *proh-muh-nahd*
promise *n.,* promesse (f) *proh-mess*
prompt, prompt *prohñ*
pronunciation, prononciation (f) *proh-nohñ-syah-syohñ*
proof, preuve (f) *próev*
proper, propre *prohpr*
property, propriété (f) *proh-pree-yeh-teh*
proposal, proposition (f) *proh-poh-zee-syohñ*
proprietor, propriétaire *proh-pree-yeh-ter*

prosperity, prospérité (f) *proh-speh-ree-teh*
protect, protéger *proh-teh-zheh*
protection, protection (f) *proh-tek-syohñ*
protestant, protestant *proh-tes-tahñ*
proud, fier, orgueilleux *fyer, or-géù-eh-yóè*
provide, fournir *foor-neer*
province, province (f) *proh-vañss*
provincial, provincial *proh-vañ-syal*
provision, préparatifs (m, pl) *preh-pa-ra-teef*
prune, pruneau (m) *préù-noh*
public, public *péùb-leek*
publish, publier *péùb-lee-yeh*
pull *v.,* tirer *tee-reh*
pump, pompe (f) *pohñmp*
punish, punir *péù-neer*
purchase *n.,* achat (m), emplette (f) *ah-shah, ahñm-plet*
pure, pur *péùr*
purple, pourpre *poorpr*
purpose *n.,* but (m) *béù*
purse, bourse (f) *boorss*
purser, commissaire (m) *ko-mee-ser*
push *v.,* pousser *poo-seh*
put, mettre *metr* [74]

quality, qualité (f) *ka-lee-teh*
quantity, quantité (f) *kahñ-tee-teh*
quarrel *n.,* querelle (f) *ke-rel*
quarrel *v.,* quereller *ke-ruh-leh*
quarter *adj. & n.,* quart (m) *kar*
queen, reine (f) *ren*
question *n.,* question (f) *kes-tyohñ*
quick, rapide, vite *ra-peed, veet*
quickly, vite *veet*
quiet, tranquille *trahñ-keel*
quite, complètement *kohñ-plet-mahñ*

radio, radio (f) *rah-dyoh*
railroad, chemin de fer (m) *shuh-mañ duh fer*
railroad car, wagon (m) *va-gohñ*
railroad station, gare (f) *gar* [44, 82]
rain *n.,* pluie (f) *plêu-ee* [7]
rain *v.,* pleuvoir *plôe-vwar* [5, 101]
rainbow, arc-en-ciel (m) *ark-ahñ-syel* [7]
raincoat, imperméable (m) *añm-per-meh-yabl* [6]
raise *v.,* augmenter, lever *ohg-mahñ-teh, luh-veh*
rapidly, rapidement *ra-peed-mahñ*
rare, rare *rar*
rash *n.,* éruption (f) *eh-rêup-syohñ*
raspberry, framboise (f) *frahñm-bwahz*
rate, cours (m) *koor*
rather, plutôt *plêu-toh*
raw, cru *krêu*
razor, rasoir (m) *ra-zwar*
razor blade, lame de rasoir (f) *lahm duh ra-zwar*
reach *v.,* atteindre *a-tañdr*
read, lire *leer*
ready, prêt *pre* [50, 76]
real, réel *reh-yel*
really, réellement, vraiment *reh-yel-mahñ, vre-mahñ*
rear, arrière (m) *a-ree-yer*
reason *n.,* raison (f) *re-zohñ*
reasonable, raisonnable *re-zo-nabl*
receipt, reçu (m) *ruh-sêu* [31]
receive, recevoir *ruh-suh-vwar*
recent, récent *reh-sahñ*
reception desk, réception (f) *reh-sep-syohñ*
recognize, reconnaître *ruh-ko-netr*
recommend, recommander *ruh-ko-mahñ-deh* [50]
reconfirm [a flight], reconfirmer *ruh-kohñ-feer-meh* [89]
recover, se remettre *suh ruh-metr*
red, rouge *roozh*
reduce, réduire *reh-dêu-eer*

reduction, réduction (f) *reh-dêuk-syohñ*

refreshments, rafraîchissements (m, pl) *ra-fre-shees-mahñ*

refund v., rembourser *rañm-boor-seh*

refuse v., refuser *ruh-fêu-zeh*

region, région (f) *reh-zhyohñ*

register n., registre *re-zheestr*

register [a letter], recommander *ruh-ko-mahñ-deh;* [at a hotel], enregistrer, signer le registre *ahñ-reh-zhees-treh, seen-yeh luh reh-zheestr*

regret v., regretter *ruh-gre-teh*

regular, régulier *reh-gêu-lyeh*

regulation, règle (f) *regl*

relative [kin], parent (m) *pa-rahñ*

religion, religion (f) *re-lee-zhyohñ*

remark n., remarque (f) *ruh-mark*

remember, se souvenir de, se rappeler *suh soo-vuh-neer duh, suh rap-leh*

remove, enlever *ahñ-luh-veh*

renew, renouveler *ruh-noo-vuh-leh*

rent v., louer *loo-eh*

repair v., réparer *reh-pa-reh*

repeat v., répéter *reh-peh-teh* [10]

replace [put back], remettre *ruh-metr*

reply n., réponse (f) *reh-pohñss*

republic, république (f) *reh-pêub-leek*

request v., demander *duh-mahñ-deh*

rescue v., sauver *soh-veh*

reservation, réservation (f) *reh-zer-vah-syohñ*

reserve v., réserver *reh-zer-veh* [53]

reserved, réservé *reh-zer-veh*

residence, résidence (f) *reh-zee-dahñss*

resident, résident *reh-see-dahñ*

responsible, responsable *re-spohñ-sabl*

rest n., repos (m) *ruh-poh*

rest v., se reposer *suh ruh-poh-zeh*

restaurant, restaurant (m) *re-stoh-rahñ* [37, 48]

restless, agité *a-zhee-teh*

rest room, cabinet de toilettes (m) *ka-bee-neh duh twah-let*

result *n.*, résultat (m) *reh-zeûl-tah*

return *v.*, revenir *ruh-vuh-neer*

return ticket, billet de retour (m) *bee-yeh duh ruh-toor*

review *n.*, revue (f) *ruh-veû*

reward, récompense (f) *reh-kohñ-pahñss*

rib, côte (f) *koht*

ribbon, ruban (m) *reû-bahñ*

rice, riz (m) *ree*

rich, riche *reesh*

ride *n.*, promenade (f) *proh-muh-nahd*

right [correct], correct *ko-rekt*   **to be right,** avoir raison *a-vwar re-zohñ* [12]   **all right,** très bien *tre byañ*

right [direction], droite (f) *drwaht* [44]

ring *n.*, bague (f) *bahg*

ring *v.*, sonner *so-neh* [41]

ripe, mûr *meûr*

rise *v.*, se lever *suh luh-veh*

river, rivière (f), fleuve (m) *ree-vyer, fleûv* [100, 101]

road, route (f), chemin (m) *root, shuh-mañ* [75]

roast, rôti (m) *roh-tee*

rob, voler *vo-leh* [14]

robber, voleur (m) *vo-leûr*

rock, rocher (m) *ro-sheh*

roll [bread], petit pain (m) *puh-tee pañ*

roll *v.*, rouler *roo-leh*

roof, toit (m) *twah*

room, pièce (f), chambre (f) *pyess, shahñmbr* [35, 36, 38]

rope, corde (f) *kord*

rose, rose (f) *rohz*

rouge [make up], rouge à joues (m) *roozh a zhoo*

rough, agité, rude *a-zhee-teh, reûd*

round, rond *rohñ*

round trip, aller et retour (m) *a-leh eh ruh-toor* [83]

royal, royal *rwah-yal*

rubber, caoutchouc (m) *kah-oo-choo*
rude, grossier *gro-syeh*
rug, tapis (m) *ta-pee*
ruin *v.*, ruiner *rêû-ee-neh*
rum, rhum (m) *rôêm*
run *v.*, courir *koo-reer*
runway, piste (f) *peest* [90]

sad, triste *treest*
safe, sauf *sohf*
safety pin, épingle de sûreté *eh-pañgl duh sêûr-teh*
sail *v.*, faire voile, partir *fer vwahl, par-teer* [86]
sailor, marin (m) *ma-rañ*
saint, saint *sañ*
salad, salade (f) *sa-lad*
sale, vente (f) *vahñt* [67]; [reduced prices], solde (m) *sold*
   for sale, en vente *ahn vahnt*
salesgirl, vendeuse (f) *vahñ-dôêz*
salesman, vendeur *vahñ-dôêr*
salmon, saumon (m) *soh-mohñ*
salt, sel (m) *sel*
same, même *mem* **the same as,** le même que *luh mem
   kuh*
sample *n.*, échantillon (m) *eh-shahñ-tee-yohñ*
sand, sable (m) *sabl*
sandwich, sandwich (m) *sahñd-veetch*
sanitary, sanitaire *sa-nee-ter*
sanitary napkin, serviette hygiénique (f) *ser-vee-yet ee-
   zhyeh-neek*
satin, satin (m) *sa-tañ*
satisfactory, satisfaisant *sa-tees-fe-zahñ*
satisfied, satisfait *sa-tees-fe*
satisfy, satisfaire *sa-tees-fer*
Saturday, samedi (m) *sam-dee*
sauce, sauce (f) *sohss*
saucer, soucoupe (f) *soo-koop*

sausage, saucisse (f) *soh-seess*

save [money], économiser, épargner *eh-ko-no-mee-zeh, eh-par-nyeh;* [rescue], sauver *soh-veh*

say, dire *deer* [10]

scale, échelle (f) *eh-shel*

scar *n.,* cicatrice (f) *see-ka-treess*

scarce, rare *rar*

scarcely, à peine *a pen*

scare *v.,* effrayer *e-freh-yeh*

scarf, écharpe (f), foulard (m) *eh-sharp, foo-lar*

scenery, paysage (m) *peh-ee-zahzh*

scent *n.,* odeur (f) *oh-dôer*

schedule *n.,* horaire (m) *or-er*

school, école (f) *eh-kol*

science, science (f) *see-yahñss*

scientist, savant (m) *sa-vahñ*

scissors, ciseaux (m, pl) *see-zoh*

scratch *n.,* égratignure (f) *eh-gra-teen-yêur*

sculpture, sculpture (f) *skêul-têur*

sea, mer (f) *mer*

seafood, marée (f) *ma-reh*

seagull, mouette (f) *moo-et*

seam, couture (f) *koo-têur*

seaport, port de mer (m) *por duh mer*

search *v.,* chercher *sher-sheh*

seasick, mal de mer (f) *mal duh mer* [88]

season, saison (f) *se-zohñ*

seat, siège (m) *syezh*

second, second, deuxième *suh-kohñ, dôe-zyem* **second class,** deuxième classe *dôe-zyem klass* [83]

secret *adj. & n.,* secret *se-kre*

secretary, secrétaire (m, f) *se-kreh-ter*

section, section (f) *sek-syohñ*

see, voir *vwar* [7, 98]

seem, sembler *sahñm-bleh*

select *v.,* choisir *shwah-zeer*

selection, choix (m) *shwah*
self, même *mem*
sell, vendre *vahñdr* [63, 69]
send, envoyer *ahñ-vwah-yeh* [11, 69]
sensible, raisonnable *re-zo-nabl*
separate *adj.,* séparé *seh-pa-reh*
separate *v.,* séparer *seh-pa-reh*
September, septembre (m) *sep-tahñmbr*
series, série (f) *seh-ree*
serious, sérieux *seh-ree-yöe*
servant, domestique (m, f) *do-mehs-teek*
serve *v.,* servir *ser-veer* [50, 63, 89]
service, service (m) *ser-veess* **service charge,** frais de
    service (m, pl) *fre duh ser-veess*
set [fixed], arrangé *a-rahñ-zheh*
set [place] *v.,* arranger *a-rahñ-zheh*
seven, sept *set*
seventeen, dix-sept *deess-set*
seventh, septième *se-tyem*
seventy, soixante-dix *swah-sahñt deess*
several, plusieurs *plöe-zyöer*
severe, sévère *seh-ver*
sew, coudre *koodr*
shade, ombre (f) *ohñmbr*
shampoo, shampooing (m) *shahñm-poo-eeng*
shape *n.,* forme (f) *form*
share *v.,* partager *par-ta-zheh*
shark, requin (m) *ruh-kañ*
sharp, aigu *e-géü*
shave *v.,* raser, se raser *ra-zeh, suh ra-zeh*
shaving cream, savon à raser *sa-vohñ a ra-zeh*
she, elle *el*
sheep, mouton (m) *moo-tohñ*
sheet [bedsheet], drap (m) *drah;* [leaf], feuille (f) *föe-eey*
shellfish, coquillage (m) *ko-kee-yahzh*
shelter, abri (m) *a-bree*

sherry, xéres (m) *sheh-reh*

shine *v.,* briller *bree-yeh*

ship *n.,* bateau (m), navire (m) *ba-toh, na-veer* [86, 88]

ship *v.,* expédier *ek-speh-dyeh* [69]

shirt, chemise (f) *shuh-meez* [38, 68]

shiver *v.,* frissonner *free-so-neh*

shock *n.,* choc (m) *shok*

shoe, chaussure (f), soulier (m) *shoh-sēur, soo-lyeh* [68]

shoelaces, lacets (m, pl) *lah-seh*

shoeshine, cirer les souliers *see-reh leh soo-lyeh*

shoestore, magasin de chaussures (m) *ma-ga-zañ duh shoh-sēur*

shoot *v.,* tirer *tee-reh*

shop *n.,* magasin (m), boutique (f) *ma-ga-zañ, boo-teek*

shop [to go shopping], faire des achats, faire des emplettes *fer deh zah-shah, fer deh zahñm-plet* [61]

shopping center, centre d'achats (m) *sahñtr dah-shah* [101]

shore, rivage (m) *ree-vahzh*

short, court *koor* [68]

shorts, caleçon (m) *kal-sohñ*

shoulder, épaule (f) *eh-pohl*

show *n.,* spectacle (m) *spek-takl*

show *v.,* montrer *mohñ-treh* [11, 66, 92]

shower [bath], douche (f) *doosh* [36]

shrimp, crevette (f) *kruh-vet*

shut *adj.,* fermé *fer-meh*

shut *v.,* fermer *fer-meh*

shy, timide *tee-meed*

sick, malade *ma-lad* [92]

side, côté (m) *koh-teh*

sidewalk, trottoir (m) *tro-twar*

sight, vue (f) *vēu*

sightseeing, tourisme (m), visite des curiosités (f) *toor-eezm, vee-zeet deh kēu-ree-yo-zee-teh* [97]

sign *n.,* enseigne (f) *ahñ-seny*

sign *v.,* signer *see-nyeh* [31]

signature, signature (f) *see-nya-tếûr*
silence, silence (m) *see-lahñss*
silent, silencieux *see-lahñ-syốè*
silk, soie (f) *swah*
silly, stupide *stếû-peed*
silver, argent (m) *ar-zhahñ*
similar, semblable *sahñm-blabl*
simple, simple *sañmpl*
since, depuis *duh-pếû-ee*
sing, chanter *shahñ-teh*
single, seul *sốèl*
sir, monsieur *muh-syốè*
sister, soeur (f) *sốèr* [2]
sit, s'asseoir *sa-swar* [99]
situation, situation (f) *see-tếû-ah-syohñ*
six, six *seess*
sixteen, seize *sez*
sixth, sixième *see-zyem*
sixty, soixante *swah-sahñt*
size, taille (f), grandeur (f) *tah-eey, grahñ-dốèr* [66]
skillful, adroit, habile *a-drwah, a-beel*
skin, peau (f) *poh*
skirt, jupe (f) *zhếûp* [68]
skull, crâne (m) *krahn*
sky, ciel (m) *syel*
sleep *n.,* sommeil (m) *so-meh-eey*
sleep *v.,* dormir *dor-meer* [95]
sleeve, manche (f) *mahñsh* [68]
slice *n.,* tranche (f) *trahñsh*
slice *v.,* découper en tranches *deh-koo-peh ahñ trahñsh*
slight, léger *leh-zheh*
slip [garment], jupon (m) *zhếû-pohñ*
slip *v.,* glisser *glee-seh*
slippers, pantoufles (f, pl) *pahñ-toofl*
slippery, glissant *glee-sahñ* [75]
slow, lent *lahñ*

slowly, lentement *lahñt-mahñ* [10, 44]

small, petit *puh-tee*

smart, intelligent *añ-te-lee-zhahñ*

smell *n.*, odeur (f) *o-döer*

smell *v.*, sentir *sahñ-teer*

smile *n.*, sourire (m) *soo-reer*

smile *v.*, sourire *soo-reer*

smoke *n.*, fumée (f) *fêu-meh*

smoke *v.*, fumer *fêu-meh* [89, 94]

smooth, lisse *leess*

snack, casse-croûte (m) *kas-kroot*

snow, neige (f) *nezh* **it's snowing,** il neige *eel nezh*

so, ainsi, alors, si *añ-see, a-lor, see* **so that,** de manière que, afin que *duh ma-nyer kuh, a-fañ kuh*

soap, savon (m) *sa-vohñ* [39]

social, social *so-syal*

sock, chaussette (f) *shoh-set*

soda, soda (m) *so-dah*

soft, mou *moo*

sold, vendu *vahñ-dêu*

solid, solide *so-leed*

some, quelque *kel-kuh*

somehow, de façon ou d'autre *duh fa-sohñ oo dohtr*

someone, quelqu'un *kel-kôeñ*

something, quelque chose *kel-kuh shohz*

sometimes, quelquefois *kel-kuh-fwah*

somewhere, quelque part *kel-kuh par*

son, fils (m) *feess* [2]

song, chanson (f) *shahñ-sohñ*

soon, bientôt *byañ-toh*

sore *adj.*, douloureux *doo-loo-rôe*

sore throat, mal à la gorge *mal a la gorzh*

sorrow, chagrin (m) *sha-grañ*

sorry, affligé *a-flee-zheh* **to be sorry,** regretter *ruh-gre-teh* **I'm sorry,** je regrette *zhuh ruh-gret*

sort, sorte (f) *sort*

soul, âme (m) *ahm*

sound *n.*, son (m) *sohñ*

soup, potage (m), soupe (f) *po-tahzh, soop* [53]

sour, aigre *egr* [52]

south, sud (m) *sêud*

southeast, sud-est *sêud-est*

southwest, sud-ouest *sêud-oo-est*

souvenir, souvenir (m) *soo-vuh-neer*

space, espace (m) *e-spahss*

speak, parler *par-leh* [10]   **do you speak English?** parlez-vous anglais? *par-leh voo ahñ-gle*

special, spécial *speh-syal*

specialty, spécialité (f) *speh-syal-ee-teh*

speed, vitesse (f) *vee-tess* [75]

spell *v.*, épeler *ehp-leh*

spend [money], dépenser *deh-pahñ-seh;* [time], passer *pah-seh*

spicy, piquant *pee-kahñ*

spinach, épinards (m, pl) *eh-pee-nar*

spine, épine dorsale (f) *eh-peen-dor-sal*

splendid, splendide *splahñ-deed*

spoiled, gâté *gah-teh*

spoon, cuillère (f) *kêu-ee-yer* [54]

spot *n.*, tache (f) *tash*

sprain *n.*, entorse (f) *ahñ-torss*

spring, [water], source (f) *soorss*

spring [season], printemps (m) *prañ-tahñ*

springs [of a car], ressorts (m, pl) *ruh-sor*

square *adj.*, carré *ka-reh*

square [public], place (f) *plass* [99]

stairs, escalier (m) *e-ska-lyeh*

stamp, timbre-poste (m) *tañmbr-post* [39]

stand *v.*, être debout *etr duh-boo*

star, étoile (f) *eh-twahl* [7]

starch, amidon (m) *a-mee-dohñ*

start *n.*, commencement (m) *ko-mahñss-mahñ*

start v., commencer *ko-mahñ-seh*

state, état (m) *eh-tah*

stateroom, cabine (f) *ka-been* [87]

station, gare (f) *gar* [82]

statue, statue (f) *sta-téü*

stay v., rester *re-steh* [15, 37]; [lodge], loger *lo-zheh*

steak, bifteck (m) *beef-tek*

steal v., voler *vo-leh* [14]

steel, acier (m) *a-syeh*

steep, escarpé *es-kar-peh*

step, pas (m) *pah*

stew, ragoût (m) *ra-goo*

steward, garçon de cabine (m) *gar-sohñ duh ka-been* [87]

stick n., bâton (m) *bah-tohñ*

stiff, raide *red*

still [quiet], silencieux *see-lahñ-syöè*

still [yet], encore *ahñ-kor*

sting n., piqûre (f) *pee-kêur*

sting v., piquer *pee-keh*

stocking, bas (m) *bah*

stolen, volé *vo-leh*

stomach, estomac (m) *e-sto-mah* [92]

stone, pierre (f) *pyer*

stop n., arrêt (m) *a-re*

stop v., s'arrêter *sa-re-teh* [13, 44, 45, 84]

store n., magasin (m), boutique (f) *ma-ga-zañ, boo-teek* [61, 63, 98]

storey, étage *eh-tahzh*

storm, tempête (f), orage (m) *tahñm-pet, o-rahzh*

story, histoire (f) *ees-twar*

straight, droit *drwah*

straight ahead, tout droit *too drwah* [44]

strange, étrange *eh-trahñzh*

stranger, étranger *eh-trahñ-zheh*

strawberry, fraise (f) *frez*

stream, courant (m), ruisseau (m) *koo-rahñ, réü-ee-soh*

street, rue (f) *réu* [36, 45, 99, 100]
strength, force (f) *forss*
string, ficelle (f) *fee-sel*
strong, fort *for*
structure, structure (f) *stréuk-téur*
student, étudiant *eh-téu-dyahñ*
study v., étudier *eh-téu-dyeh*
style, style (m) *steel*
suburb, faubourg (m), banlieue (f) *foh-boor, bahñ-lyóe*
subway, métro (m) *meh-troh*
succeed [follow], suivre *séu-eevr,* [attain one's goal],
   réussir *reh-éu-seer*
success, succès (m) *séuk-se*
such, tel *tel*
suddenly, subitement, tout à coup, tout d'un coup *séu-
   beet-mahñ, toot a koo, too dóeñ koo*
suffer, souffrir *soo-freer*
sufficient, suffisant *séu-fee-zahñ*
sugar, sucre (m) *séukr* [50, 51, 52]
suggest, suggérer *séug-zheh-reh*
suggestion, suggestion (f) *séug-zhes-tyohñ*
suit [for men], complet (m) *kohñm-ple;* [for women],
   tailleur (m) *tah-ee-yóer*
suitcase, valise (m) *valeez* [38]
summer, été, (m) *eh-teh*
sun, soleil (m), *so-lehy* [67]
sunburned, brûlé par le soleil *bréu-leh par luh so-lehy*
Sunday, dimanche (m) *dee-mahñsh*
sunglasses, lunettes contre le soleil *léu-net kohñtr luh
   so-lehy*
sunny, ensoleillé *ahñ-so-leh-yeh*
supper, souper (m) *soo-peh* [48]
sure, sûr *séur*
surface, superficie (f) *séu-per-fee-see*
surprise n., surprise (f) *séur-preez*
surprise v., surprendre *séur-prahñdr*

suspect *v.*, soupçonner *soop-so-neh*
suspicion, soupçon (m) *soop-sohñ*
sweater, chandail (m) *shahñ-dah-eey* [6]
sweep, balayer *ba-leh-yeh*
sweet, doux *doo*
swim *v.*, nager *nah-zheh* [101]
swollen, enflé *ahñ-fleh*
sword, épée (f) *eh-peh*

table, table (f) *tabl* [50, 53, 56, 87]
tablecloth, nappe (f) *nap* [56]
tail, queue (f) *kôè*
tailor, tailleur (m) *tah-ee-yôèr*
take, prendre *prahñdr* **take off**, ôter, enlever *oh-teh, ahñ-luh-veh*
talk, parler *par-leh*
tall, grand *grahñ*
tank, réservoir (m) *reh-zer-vwar*
taste *n.*, goût (m) *goo*
taste *v.*, goûter *goo-teh*
tax *n.*, taxe (f), impôt (m) *taks, añm-poh*
taxi, taxi (m) *tak-see* [43]
tea, thé (m) *teh* [52]
teach, enseigner *ahñ-se-nyeh*
teacher, maître (m), instituteur (m) *metr, añ-stee-tûù-tôèr*
tear [drop], larme (f) *larm*
tear *v.*, déchirer *deh-shee-reh*
teaspoon, petite cuillère (f) *puh-teet kêù-ee-yer*
teeth, dents (f, pl) *dahñ*
telegram, télégramme (m) *teh-leh-grahm*
telephone, téléphone (m) *teh-leh-fon* [40]
telephone booth, cabine téléphonique (f) *ka-been teh-leh-fo-neek*
telephone operator, téléphoniste (f) *teh-leh-fon-eest*
television, télévision (f) *teh-leh-vee-zyohñ*
tell, dire, raconter *deer, ra-kohñ-teh* [11, 45]

temperature, température (f) *tahñm-peh-rah-téùr*
temple, temple (m) *tahñmpl*
temporary, temporaire *tahñm-poh-rer*
ten, dix *dees*
tent, tente (f) *tahñt*
tenth, dixième *dee-zyem*
test, examen (m) *eg-za-mañ*
than, que *kuh*
thank, remercier *ruh-mer-syeh*   **thank you,** merci *mer-see*
thankful, reconnaissant *ruh-ko-ne-sahñ*
that *conj.,* que *kuh*
that *pron.,* cela, ça, ce, cet, cette *suh-la, sa, suh, set, set*
the, le (m), la (f), les (pl) *luh, la, leh*
theater, théâtre (m) *teh-ahtr* [100]
theft, vol (m) *vol*
their, leur *lőèr*
theirs, le leur *luh lőèr*
them, les, leur *leh, lőèr*
then, alors, donc *a-lor, dohñk*
there *adv.,* là, y *la, ee*   **there is, there are,** il y a *eel ee a*
therefore, par conséquent *par kohñ-seh-kahñ*
thermometer, thermomètre (m) *ter-moh-metr*
these *adj.,* ces *seh*
these *pron.,* ceux-ci *sőè-see*
they, ils *eel*
thick, épais *eh-pe*
thief, voleur (m) *vo-lőèr*
thigh, cuisse (f) *kéù-eess*
thin, mince, maigre *mañss, megr*
thing, chose (f) *shohz*
think, penser *pahñ-seh*
third, troisième *trwah-zyem*
thirst, soif (f) *swahf*
thirsty: to be thirsty, avoir soif *a-vwar swahf* [47, 48]
thirteen, treize *trez*
thirty, trente *trahñt*

this *adj.*, ce, cet, cette *suh, set, set*

this *pron.*, ceci, celui-ci, celle-ci *suh-see, suh-léû-ee-see, sel-see*

those *adj.*, ces, ces . . . la *seh, seh . . . la*

those *pron.*, ceux, celles, ceux-la, celles-la *sôê, sel, sôê-la, sel-la*

thoroughfare, voie de communication (f) *vwah duh ko-méû-nee-kah-syohñ*

thousand, mille *meel*

thread, fil (m) *feel* [69]

three, trois *trwah*

throat, gorge (f) *gorzh*

through *prep.*, à travers *a tra-ver*

through [finished], fini *fee-nee*

throw, lancer, jeter *lahñ-seh, zhuh-teh*

thumb, pouce (m) *pooss*

thunder, tonnerre (m) *to-ner*

Thursday, jeudi (m) *zhôê-dee*

ticket, billet (m) *bee-yeh* [83, 85, 89]

ticket office, guichet (m) *gee-sheh* [83]

tie [bind], attacher, lier *a-ta-sheh, lee-yeh*

tight, serré *se-reh* [69]

tighten, serrer *se-reh*

till, jusqu'à *zhêûs-ka*

time, temps (m), fois (f) *tahñ, fwah* **what time is it?** quelle heure est-il? *kel ôer e-teel* **on time,** à l'heure *a lôer*

timetable, horaire (m) *or-er* [83]

tip [money], pourboire (m) *poor-bwar* [56]

tire [of a car], pneu (m) *pnôê* **flat tire,** pneu crevé *pnôê kruh-veh*

tire *v.*, se fatiguer *suh fa-tee-geh*

tired, fatigué *fa-tee-geh* [99]

to, à *a*

toast, pain grillé *pañ gree-yeh*

tobacco, tabac (m) *tah-bah* [33]

tobacconist, marchand de tabac (m) *mar-shahñ duh tah-bah*

today, aujourd'hui *oh-zhoor-déu-ee* [93]

toe, orteil (m) *or-tehy*

together, ensemble *ahñ-sahñmbl*

toilet, toilette (f), cabinet (m) *twah-let, ka-bee-neh*

toilet paper, papier hygiénique (m) *pa-pyeh ee-zhyeh-neek*

tomato, tomate (f) *to-mat*

tomorrow, demain *duh-mañ* [3, 96]

tongue, langue (f) *lahñg* [92]

tonight, ce soir *suh swar*

tonsils, amygdales (f, pl) *a-meeg-dal*

too [excessive], trop *troh;* [also], aussi *oh-see*

tooth, dent (f) *dahñ*

toothache, mal aux dents (m) *mal oh dahñ*

toothbrush, brosse à dents (f) *bross a dahñ*

toothpaste, pâte dentifrice *paht dahñ-tee-freess*

top, sommet (m) *so-meh*

torn, déchiré *deh-shee-reh*

total, total (m) *to-tal*

touch v., toucher *too-sheh*

tough, dur *déur*

tour, tour (m) *toor* [98, 101]

tow, remorquer *ruh-mor-keh*

toward, vers *ver*

towel, serviette (f), essuie-mains (m) *ser-vee-yet, e-séu-ee-mañ* [39]

town, ville (f) *veel*

toy, jouet (m) *zhoo-eh*

toy shop, magasin de jouets (m) *ma-ga-zañ duh zhoo-eh*

trade, commerce (m) *ko-merss*

traffic, circulation (f) *seer-kéu-lah-syohñ*

train n., train (m) *trañ* [14, 82, 83, 84, 85]

transfer v., transférer *trahñ-feh-reh* [46]

translate, traduire *tra-déu-eer*

translation, traduction (f) *tra-déuk-syohñ*

translator, traducteur (m) *tra-déŭk-tŏer*

transmission, transmission (f) *trahñz-mee-syohñ*

transportation, transport (m) *trahñs-por*

travel *v.,* voyager *vwah-yah-zheh*

traveler, voyageur (m) *vwah-yah-zhŏer*

traveler's check, chèque de voyageurs (m) *shek duh vwah-yah-zhŏer* [30]

tray, plateau (m) *pla-toh*

tree, arbre (m) *arbr*

trip, voyage (m) *vwah-yahzh* [88]

tropical, tropical *tro-pee-kal*

trousers, pantalon (m) *pahñ-ta-lohñ*

truck, camion (m) *ka-myohñ*

true, vrai *vre*

trunk, malle (f) *mal*

truth, vérité (f) *veh-rec-teh*

try *v.,* essayer *e-seh-yeh* **try on,** essayer *e-seh-yeh* [66]

Tuesday, mardi (m) *mar-dee*

turn *n.,* virage (m) *vee-rahzh*

turn *v.,* (se) tourner *(suh) toor-neh* [44]

twelve, douze *dooz*

twenty, vingt *vañ*

twice, deux fois *dŏe fwah*

twin beds, lits jumeaux (m, pl) *lee zhĕŭ-moh*

two, deux *dŏe*

ugly, laid *le*

umbrella, parapluie (m) *pa-ra-plĕŭ-ee* [6]

uncle, oncle (m) *ohñkl*

uncomfortable, incommode *añ-ko-mod*

unconscious, inconscient *añ-kohñ-syahñ*

under *prep.,* sous *soo*

underneath *prep.,* au-dessous de *oh-duh-soo duh*

undershirt, chemisette (f), gilet de dessous (m) *shuh-mee-zet, zhee-leh duh duh-soo*

understand, comprendre *kohñm-prahñdr* [10]

underwear, sous-vêtement (m) *soo-vet-mahñ*
undress *v.,* se déshabiller *suh deh-za-bee-yeh*
unequal, inégal *een-eh-gal*
unfair, injuste *añ-zhêûst*
unfortunate, malheureux *mal-ôe-rôe*
unhappy, malheureux *mal-ôe-rôe*
unhealthy, malsain *mal-sañ*
United States, États-Unis (m) *eh-ta-zêû-nee*
university, université (f) *êû-nee-ver-see-teh*
unless, à moins que *a mwañ kuh*
unlucky, infortuné *ang-for-têû-neh*
unpack, déballer *deh-ba-leh*
unpleasant, désagréable *deh-za-greh-yabl*
unsafe, dangereux *dahñ-zhuh-rôe*
until, jusqu'à, jusqu'à ce que *zhêûs-ka, zhêûs-ka suh kuh*
untrue, faux *foh*
unusual, rare *rar*
up, haut, en haut *oh, ahñ oh*
upper, supérieur *sêû-peh-ree-yôer*
upstairs, en haut *ahñ oh*
urgent, urgent *eur-zhahñ*
us, nous *noo*
use *n.,* emploi *ahñm-plwah*
use *v.,* utiliser, employer *êû-tee-lee-zeh, ahñ-plwah-yeh*
useful, utile *êû-teel*
useless, inutile *een-êû-teel*
usual, habituel *a-bee-têû-el*

vacant, libre *leebr*
vacation, vacances (f, pl) *va-kahñss*
vaccination, vaccination (f) *vak-see-nah-syohñ*
valuable, précieux *preh-syôe*
value *n.,* valeur (f) *va-lôer*
vanilla, vanille (f) *va-neey*
variety, variété (f) *va-ree-yeh-teh*
veal, veau (m) *voh*

vegetables, légumes (m) *leh-gēum*

very, très *tre*

vest, gilet (m) *zhee-leh*

victim, victime (f) *veek-teem*

view *n.*, vue (f) *vēu* [36]

village, village (m) *vee-lahzh*

vinegar, vinaigre (m) *veen-egr*

visa *n.*, visa (m) *vee-za*

visit *n.*, visite (f) *vee-zeet*

visit *v.*, visiter *vee-zee-teh* [98, 100]

voice, voix (f) *vwah*

voyage *n.*, voyage (m) *vwah-yahzh*

waist, taille (f) *tah-eey*

wait *v.*, attendre *a-tahñdr* [11, 22, 44]

waiter, garçon (m) *gar-sohñ* [50, 56]

waiting room, salle d'attente (f) *sal da-tahñt* [85]

waitress, serveuse (f) *ser-vōez* [50]

wake up, éveiller, se réveiller *eh-veh-yeh, suh reh-veh-yeh* [39]

walk *n.*, promenade (f) *proh-muh-nahd*

walk *v.*, marcher *mar-sheh* [99]

wall, mur (m) *mēur*

wallet, portefeuille (m) *port-fōe-eey*

want *v.*, vouloir *vool-war* **I want,** je veux *zhuh vōe*

warm, chaud *shoh* [4, 52, 55]

warn, avertir *a-ver-teer*

warning, avertissement (m) *a-ver-tees-mahñ*

wash *v.*, se laver *suh la-veh* [38, 74]

wasp, guêpe (f) *gep*

watch *n.*, montre (f) *mohñtr*

watch *v.*, regarder *ruh-gar-deh*

water, eau (f) *oh* [6, 51, 74, 101]

waterfall, chute d'eau (f) *shēut doh*

wave [ocean], vague (f) *vahg*

way, [manner], façon (f) *fa-sohñ*

we, nous *noo*
weak, faible *febl*
wear *v.*, porter *por-teh*
weather, temps (m) *tahñ* [4, 6]
Wednesday, mercredi (m) *mer-kruh-dee*
week, semaine (f) *suh-men* [37]
weigh, peser *pe-zeh*
weight, poids (m) *pwah*
welcome *n.*, accueil (m) *akeû-ehy*
well, bien *byan* **well done** [food], bien cuit *byan keû-ee;* [act], bien fait *byañ fe*
well [for water], puits (m) *peû-ee*
west, ouest (m) *oo-est*
wet, mouillé *moo-ee-eh*
what *interr.*, que? *kuh* **what else?** quoi encore? *kwah ahñ-kor*
wheel, roue (f) *roo*
when, quand, lorsque *kahñ, lors-kuh*
where, où *oo* **where is?** où est? *oo e* **where are?** où sont? *oo sohñ?*
wherever, n'importe où *nañm-portoo*
which *interr.*, quel? *kel*
while, pendant que *pahñ-dahñ kuh*
whip *n.*, fouet (m) *foo-eh*
white, blanc *blahñ* [68]
who *interr.*, qui? *kee*
who *rel.*, qui *kee*
whole, entier *ahñ-tyeh*
whom *interr.*, qui *kee*
whose *interr.*, à qui? *a kee*
why *interr.*, pourquoi? *poor-kwah*
wide, large *larzh* [68]
width, largeur (f) *lar-zhoer*
wife, femme *fam* [2]
wild, sauvage *soh-vahzh*
willing, vouloir bien *vool-war byañ*

win *v.*, gagner *ga-nyeh*

wind, vent (m) *vahñ* [5]

window, fenêtre (f) *fuh-netr* [38, 84]

windshield, pare-brise (m) *par-breez* [76]

wine, vin (m) *vañ* [54, 55] **white wine**, vin blanc *vañ blahñ* **red wine**, vin rouge *vañ roozh*

wing, aile (f) *ehl*

winter, hiver (m) *ee-ver*

wipe, essuyer *e-sêû-ee-yeh*

wise, sage *sahzh*

wish *n.*, souhait (m), désir (m), voeu (m) *soo-e, deh-zeer, vôè*

wish *v.*, souhaiter, désirer *soo-e-teh, deh-zee-reh*

with, avec *a-vek*

without, sans *sahñ*

woman, femme *fam* [9]

wonderful, merveilleux *mer-veh-yôè*

wood, bois (m) *bwah*

woods, bois (m) *bwah*

wool, laine (f) *len*

word, mot (m), parole (f) *moh, pa-rol*

work *n.*, travail (m) *tra-vah-eey*

work *v.*, travailler *tra-vah-ee-yeh*

world, monde (m) *mohñd*

worried, inquiet *añ-kyeh*

worse, pire *peer*

worth, valeur (f) *va-lôèr*

wound [injury], blessure (f) *ble-sêûr*

wrap *v.*, envelopper *ahñ-vlo-peh* [69]

wrist, poignet (m) *pwah-nyeh*

wristwatch, montre-bracelet *mohntr-bra-suh-leh*

write, écrire *eh-kreer* [11, 29]

writing, écriture (f) *eh-kree-têûr*

wrong, faux, fausse, tort *foh, fohss, tor* **to be wrong**, avoir tort, être mal *a-vwahr tor, etr mal*

x-ray, rayons *X* (pl) *reh-yohñ eeks*

yard, cour (f) *koor*
year, année (f), an (m) *a-neh, ahñ* [89]
yellow, jaune *zhohn*
yes, oui, si *wee, see*
yesterday, hier *yer*
yet, encore *ahñ-kor*
you, vous, tu *voo, têu*
young, jeune *zhôèn*
your, ton (m), ta (f), votre (sing), vos (pl) *ton, ta, votr, voh*

zero, zéro (m) *zeh-roh*
zipper, fermeture éclair (f) *fer-muh-têur eh-kler*

CONVERSION TABLES

Length

1 centimètre (cm) = 0.39 inch
1 mètre (m) = 39.36 inches
1 kilomètre (km) = 0.62 mile
1 inch = 2.54 cm.
1 foot = 0.30 m.
1 mile = 1.61 km.

Weight

1 gramme (gm) = 0.04 ounce
1 kilo (kg) = 2.20 pounds
1 ounce = 28.35 gm.
1 pound = 453.59 gm.

Volume

1 litre = 0.91 dry quart
1 litre = 1.06 liquid quarts
1 pint liquid = 0.47 liter
1 US quart liquid = 0.95 liter
1 US gallon = 3.78 liters

Temperature

Celsius (°C):	−17.8	0	10	20	30	37	37.8	100
Fahrenheit (°F):	0	32	50	68	86	98.6	100	212